Samuel Smith Harris

The relation of Christianity to civil society

Samuel Smith Harris

The relation of Christianity to civil society

ISBN/EAN: 9783337263393

Printed in Europe, USA, Canada, Australia, Japan

Cover: Foto ©Lupo / pixelio.de

More available books at **www.hansebooks.com**

The Bohlen Lectures, 1882

THE

RELATION OF CHRISTIANITY

TO

CIVIL SOCIETY

BY

SAMUEL SMITH HARRIS, D.D., LL.D.
Bishop of Michigan

---

*DELIVERED IN THE CHURCH OF THE HOLY TRINITY,
PHILADELPHIA, IN ADVENT, 1882*

NEW YORK
THOMAS WHITTAKER
2 AND 3 BIBLE HOUSE
1883

COPYRIGHT, 1883,
BY THOMAS WHITTAKER.

Franklin Press:
RAND, AVERY, AND COMPANY,
BOSTON.

THE JOHN BOHLEN LECTURESHIP.

JOHN BOHLEN, who died in this city on the twenty-sixth day of April, 1874, bequeathed to trustees a fund of One Hundred Thousand Dollars, to be distributed to religious and charitable objects in accordance with the well-known wishes of the testator.

By a deed of trust, executed June 2, 1875, the trustees, under the will of Mr. BOHLEN, transferred and paid over to "The Rector, Church Wardens, and Vestrymen of the Church of the Holy Trinity, Philadelphia," in trust, a sum of money for certain designated purposes, out of which fund the sum of Ten Thousand Dollars was set apart for the endowment of THE JOHN BOHLEN LECTURESHIP, upon the following terms and conditions : —

"The money shall be invested in good, substantial, and safe securities, and held in trust for a fund to be called The John Bohlen Lectureship; and the income shall be applied annually to the payment of a qualified person, whether clergyman or layman, for the delivery and publication of at least one hundred copies of two or more lecture sermons. These lectures shall be delivered at such time and place, in the city of Philadelphia, as the persons nominated to appoint the lecturer shall from time to time determine, giving at least six-months' notice to the person appointed to deliver the same, when the same may conveniently be done, and in no case selecting the same person as lecturer a second time within a period of five years. The payment shall be made to said lecturer, after the lectures have been printed, and received by the trustees, of all the income for the year derived from said fund, after defraying the expense of printing the lectures, and the other incidental expenses attending the same.

"The subject of such lectures shall be such as is within the terms set forth in the will of the Rev. John Bampton, for the delivery of what are known as the 'Bampton Lectures,' at Oxford, or any other subject distinctively connected with or relating to the Christian Religion.

"The lecturer shall be appointed annually in the month of May, or as soon thereafter as can conveniently be done, by the persons who for the time being shall hold the offices of Bishop of the Protestant Episcopal Church of the Diocese in which is the Church of the Holy Trinity; the Rector of said Church; the Professor of Biblical Learning, the Professor of Systematic Divinity, and the Professor of Ecclesiastical History, in the Divinity School of the Protestant Episcopal Church in Philadelphia.

"In case either of said offices are vacant, the others may nominate the lecturer."

Under this trust the Right Reverend SAMUEL SMITH HARRIS, D.D., LL.D., Bishop of the Diocese of Michigan, was appointed to deliver the lectures for the year 1882.

PHILADELPHIA, ADVENT, 1882.

CONTENTS.

LECTURE I.

THE QUESTION STATED 9

"Then went the Pharisees, and took counsel how they might entangle him in his talk. And they sent out unto him their disciples with the Herodians, saying, Master, we know that thou art true, and teachest the way of God in truth, neither carest thou for any man: for thou regardest not the person of men. Tell us therefore, What thinkest thou? Is it lawful to give tribute unto Cæsar, or not?"

ST. MATTHEW xxii. 15-17.

LECTURE II.

THE ANSWER OF CHRIST, AND THE DEVELOPMENTS OF EUROPEAN HISTORY 37

"But Jesus perceived their wickedness, and said, Why tempt ye me, ye hypocrites? Shew me the tribute money. And they brought unto him a penny. And he saith unto them, Whose is this image and superscription? They say unto him, Cæsar's. Then saith he unto them, Render therefore unto Cæsar the things which are Cæsar's; and unto God the things that are God's."

ST. MATTHEW xxii. 18-21.

LECTURE III.

THE ANSWER OF CHRIST, AND THE DEVELOPMENTS OF AMERICAN HISTORY 79

"If thou let this man go, thou art not Cæsar's friend."

ST. JOHN xix. 12.

LECTURE IV.

EDUCATION 123

"And Jesus came and spake unto them, saying, All power is given unto me in heaven and in earth. Go ye therefore, and teach all nations, baptizing them in the name of the Father, and of the Son, and of the Holy Ghost: teaching them to observe all things whatsoever I have commanded you: and, lo, I am with you alway, even unto the end of the world."

ST. MATTHEW xxviii. 18–20.

LECTURE V.

CHARITY 159

"For ye have the poor with you always, and whensoever ye will ye may do them good."

ST. MARK xiv. 7.

LECTURE VI.

THE ULTIMATE ISSUE 199

"Pilate therefore said unto him, Art thou a king then? Jesus answered, Thou sayest that I am a king. To this end was I born, and for this cause came I into the world, that I should bear witness unto the truth. Every one that is of the truth heareth my voice."

ST. JOHN xviii. 37.

LECTURE I.

THE QUESTION STATED.

THE RELATION OF CHRISTIANITY

TO

CIVIL SOCIETY.

LECTURE I.

THE QUESTION STATED.

"Then went the Pharisees, and took counsel how they might entangle him in his talk. And they sent out unto him their disciples with the Herodians, saying, Master, we know that thou art true, and teachest the way of God in truth, neither carest thou for any man: for thou regardest not the person of men. Tell us therefore, What thinkest thou? Is it lawful to give tribute unto Cæsar, or not?" — ST. MATTHEW xxii. 15-17.

IN this passage we are told under what circumstances and with what design the question which is now to engage our thought was first proposed to the Founder of Christianity. No doubt the inquiry which the Pharisees and Herodians made was not only disingenuous, but was far more limited in its intent than ours must be. Their purpose was to betray Jesus into one of two alternative dangers in defining the attitude of what they regarded as a Jewish religious cult, toward a government that was at once foreign and despotic. Yet, whatever their purpose was, the formal reason upon which they proceeded was the obvious need that there should be some authoritative definition of the relation which Jesus intended should subsist between his teaching and the requirements of the existing government or civil society. That such a question should be propounded in some form was, indeed, inevitable. In the midst of the antagonisms, open and concealed, which agitated that restless age, neutrality in such a matter was believed to be impossible. Especially, for reasons which must hereafter engage our attention, the assumption of such neutrality would have been resented as quite intolerable in one who, like Jesus, claimed to be the anointed Prince of the house of David.

We shall have occasion hereafter to consider the answer which Jesus returned to his interlocutors, and we shall then see that such answer was not less complete than it was unexpected and surprising. For the present it may suffice to point out, in passing, that it disclosed a relation between Christianity and civil society which could hardly fail to be unsatisfactory to all parties in that day. To the secularist Herodian, not less than to the theocratic Pharisee, it indicated a *modus vivendi* between civil and ecclesiastical authority that appeared to be both unintelligible and intolerable. The antagonism between the two opposing ideas which they represented is not yet extinct, nor has the world yet learned altogether to accept the marvellous reconciliation of it that is implied in the answer of Jesus. For more than eighteen centuries of Christian history, grave problems of civil allegiance and social order have emerged along the line of the great movement which he instituted; and prophets and statesmen are still trying to find the principle which shall effect a final solution of them. I believe that the search need not be abandoned as unavailing. I believe that the Founder of Christianity himself laid down the principle which the world has so long been seeking, and that a reverent and humble search for it now will not be wholly unrewarded. With unfeigned humility I venture to-night to renew the attempt to discover and formulate that principle; believing that, upon its acknowledgment, the civil and religious well-being of our fellow-countrymen largely depends, and that we must look to the recognition of it for the development of a genuine Christian statesmanship in our land.

It is my purpose, however, to postpone to the second lecture of this series, the consideration of the teaching of Jesus on this subject, and to attempt in this preliminary lecture to define the philosophical basis upon which our inquiry is to rest. If any justification is needed for the more extended demand which this method will make upon our attention, it will be found, I venture to think, in the essential importance of our inquiry, and in the peculiar circumstances of the age, which make it both practical and timely. No discussion of such a subject can be of value that does not proceed from a philosophical basis; that is to say, from a basis or first principle that shall be, not merely indicated by authority, but established by reason. It is well seen, that the gravest interests, both of politics and religion, are awaiting at this moment the discovery of some middle ground, where they may be reconciled and harmonized. Such burning questions as those relating to religious and secular education, to labor and capital, to the standard of public morality, to the administration of justice and charity,— such are the questions that are standing in the outer court of our forum; and, if we are to try them, we must, first of all, establish some common philosophical ground where all the contesting interests may meet on equal terms. I believe that the solution of all these questions will be found in the recognition of the true relation between Christianity and civil society, and in the free action of each upon the other in that relation. But then we must, first of all, make up the pleadings, as the lawyers would say; that is to say, we must allow each side to tell its own story. We must first understand what civil society is, from a purely political stand-point, just as we shall insist on defining Christianity from a purely religious stand-point; and then we shall endeavor to indicate the relation between them.

First, then, we must determine the fundamental question, What is the State?—what is the philosophical basis of civil society? To this question there have been various answers. Considered in its relation to the Church, some of these answers have emerged in history as the characteristic views of ecclesiastical or political parties. For instance, the Papist would define the State as a creature of the Church; the Erastian would make the Church a department of the State; the Puritan would regulate the State on Church ideas; the Hobbist would rule the Church on reasons of State; the Quaker would abolish Church organization; and the Mennonite would suppress the office of the civil magistrate.[1] All these views are held in our own land and age, and we shall have occasion to discuss them hereafter in relation to some of the practical questions of the day. But manifestly this classification is not sufficiently fundamental for our present purpose. We need to inquire into the philosophical principle upon which civil society is founded. Upon what basis of authority does it rest? Is the authority of the State inherent, or derived? If derived, from whence? and how? Is the State a moral being,—a personality? or is it simply a social compact, an arrangement or organization of men, maintained in order to attain the ends which they seek to secure through such government or society?

[1] Bishop Warburton: The Alliance between Church and State, chap. iv. p. 41.

Upon the two answers to these questions, two antagonistic theories of government have been founded. The first of these would make the State the unit, so to speak; investing it with original sovereignty over the individual, and clothing it with the authority and attributes of a moral personality.[1] The other makes the individual man the unit; investing him with original sovereignty, declaring that he only has the authority and attributes of a moral personality, and resolving all civil government into a mere compact between men, entered into and maintained for certain common purposes, and in obedience to the impulses of their common nature.[2] Now, here it is to be remarked in passing, that the question is not at present whether government is or is not supported by a divine sanction. It is one of the common errors of this controversy, that the question of the divine sanction of human government

---

[1] Gladstone: The State in its Relations with the Church, pp. 37, 38. Aristotle: Politics, bk. i. chap. ii. Count De Maistre: Du Pape, pp. 208, 209, 212, 214. Machiavelli: Il Principe, chap. x. Sir Robert Filmer: Patriarcha, chap. iii. pp. 78, 141.

[2] Grotius: De Jure Belli et Pacis, I. 6, *et seq*. Hobbes: Leviathan, chap. xvii. p. 153, chap. xxi. p. 198. Locke: Of Civil Government, p. 383. Rousseau: Du Contrat social, i. 6. Burke: Reflections on the Revolution in France, ii. p. 368.

should be supposed to depend upon the definition of the philosophical basis of civil society. The argument in favor of such sanction is certainly not less strong under the social-compact hypothesis than under the theocratic hypothesis. The only question at present is, Which is the unit, — the State, or the individual man? Does the authority of the State rest upon enactment, or compact? Is civil society organized from the State downward, or from the individual upward?

The first of the views indicated above has been longest and most widely held in human history. In the ancient world it bore almost undisputed sway. It is not too much to say, that all absolute governments, all civic theocracies, all despotisms, both actual and theoretical, have rested upon its authority. The theory that man exists for the State, and not the State for man, was not more potent and unquestioned in the "practical politics" of Sparta than it was in the speculations of Plato in the "Republic" and "Laws."[1] It ruled in the Porch and the Areopagus at Athens. It justified the imperial conquests of Alexander. It

[1] Plato: Republic, bk. vi.; Laws, bk. v.

was acknowledged at Rome, not less under the Republic than under the Empire.[1] From that day to this it has continued to be the basis of all the pretensions of irresponsible authority, and the divine right of kings; and it is still held by multitudes of our contemporaries, and even of our own countrymen.[2] Nevertheless, the other theory, namely, that civil society rests upon a social compact between individuals; a theory that regards the man as first, and makes the government his agent, and not his irresponsible master; that begins with the rights of men, and exalts and dignifies the individual,—this theory, though late in emerging into history, has exercised a wide and increasing influence in human affairs. No doubt the perversion of it has more than once introduced confusion into political speculation.[3] No doubt it has been pleaded again and yet again in justification of the wildest and most revolutionary projects. Yet properly understood, and guarded by limitations, which I will endeavor in these inquiries to point out, there is no doubt, I think,

---

[1] Lactantius: Institutiones Divinæ, vi. 8.

[2] The prevalence and tendency of this theory in American politics will be pointed out in the Third Lecture.

[3] Rousseau: Du Contrat social, i. 6.

that the doctrine of compact is the true philosophical basis of civil society.

It is important to remember, that the inquiry in which we are now engaged is not historical, but metaphysical. We are not now concerned to ascertain by what particular steps in actual history any particular form of government came to be adopted; but our inquiry is, Upon what philosophical basis of authority does government in general, or civil society, rest? The phenomenon to be accounted for is civil society; and we desire to account for it, not empirically, but logically. The question really is, How would men now, or at any time, proceed, if all government were removed? upon what principle would they necessarily and logically proceed? It may be perfectly true that actual governments have been historically developed from patriarchical or despotic authority; yet, even in the case of such governments, the only rationale of their logical authority is the concept of a compact among men as individuals. Considered logically and not empirically, the elaboration of civil society could have taken place only as the act of mutually related individuals acting as moral persons; and the only moral person belonging to the human category is the individual man.[1] Considered logically and not empirically, then, the impulse towards civil society must begin with the individual man, and must derive its authority immediately from him. No other philosophical genesis of it is conceivable on the postulate that the individual man is the only moral person belonging to the human category. The affirmation of this postulate on the one hand, and the denial of it on the other, has led to what may be justly termed the most notable controversy in the whole history of human speculation. This was the issue that was involved in the contest between institutionalism and particularism in the old philosophies, and which raged in the famous conflict between Nominalism and Realism in the Middle Ages. Long before Christianity, the Platonic theory of ideas, and the idealism of Aristotle, laid the foundation for such an institutionalistic philosophy as almost excluded the notion of the responsibility of the individual. We shall see in the next lecture how the corrective

---

[1] Compare Locke: Of Civil Government, chap. viii. Compare also Sir Henry Sumner Maine: Early History of Institutions, lect. xii. pp. 354-370.

to this, which the Gospel supplied, was neutralized in large degree by the subordination of the Church to the civil power; and when, in the Middle Ages, the study of Aristotle was re-introduced into Europe by and through the Mahomedan doctors of Cordova, the School-authors eagerly adopted a modified type of the old idealism, and built up their famous doctrine of Realism, contending that universals were the only realities, and individuals nothing except as derived from them. Against this the inevitable re-action appeared in the theory of Nominalism, according to which individuals are the only realities, and universals but the figments of the mind, having no objective entity. The latest and most brilliant champion of Nominalism was William of Occam, an Englishman, who won the battle for his theory at the English universities, and became the father of English liberty, and the philosophical forerunner of the Reformation. It is easy to see how nearly related this scholastic controversy was to the political questions which have since agitated the world. Looking back upon those wordy debates, we can discern a significance in them, which, perhaps, the pedantic disputants themselves little understood. Though the postulate of Nominalism has been drafted into the service of many destructive tendencies, and needs, as we shall presently see, to be limited and controlled, yet in asserting the dignity of the individual man, and declaring that he alone is a moral and personal entity in the human category, the first step was taken towards the formulation of a true philosophy of civil society. Just as rapidly as this truth obtained the mastery, the dignity of conscience and the rights of men as men began to receive their due acknowledgment and recognition. The first blow was struck, since the conversion of Constantine, against despotism of all kinds when it was admitted that man is greater than any agent that he employs, and that governments were made for men and by men, and not men by governments and for them.

The philosophical postulate of Nominalism, however, needs to be qualified. Stated without qualification, it leads, no doubt, to all the errors of mere individualism; but, properly stated, those errors are guarded against, and, indeed, excluded. "Nominalism acknowledges only the individual as the truly existing, and claims that the universal is but an abstraction from the individual."[1] This conclusion I accept. But, then, the individual cannot be regarded as an isolated being, but must be considered as a member of a class or genus composed of like individuals. In other words, all individuals are distinguished by characteristics which indicate that they should be classified into genera, and, in the case of man, by corresponding social instincts, which move them to so group themselves together; and it is only in this association that the individual is able to realize his own completeness.[2] For instance, the individual man only is the truly existing; but it is the individual man characterized by a generic likeness to his fellow-man, and by a strong social instinct, which moves him to associate with his fellow-man, and to find his true completeness as well as his highest development and advantage in such association. With this qualification we may freely apply the postulate of Nominalism to our present purpose, and are in a position to define the philo-

---

[1] Martensen: Christian Ethics, p. 211.
[2] Martensen: Christian Ethics, p. 211. Aristotle: Politics, bk. i. chap. ii.

sophical basis of civil society. Civil society, then, rests upon a social compact between individual men acting in obedience to a law of their being, and under the impulses of their common nature. The ethical subject in this compact is the individual man: but it is man the moral and spiritual being; man made in the image of his Maker, and, however fallen, still the object of divine care; it is man distinguished by such characteristics, guided by such direction, and acting under that impulse of his nature which moves him to seek his highest good in association with his fellows,— he it is who makes and maintains that social compact with his fellows which sustains and constitutes civil society. No doubt, some of the motives to such association are derivable from mere experience; but the original impulse is found in his own nature. For man is essentially a social and political,[1] as well as a moral and intellectual, being. There is a law of his nature which impels him toward political society. He has certain well-defined faculties and capacities which not only seek, but depend, for their highest development, upon association with his fellows: and while the

[1] Aristotle: Politics, bk. i. chap. ii.

social impulse is confirmed and justified by certain obvious advantages which belong exclusively to such association, yet, in the movement toward society, his whole nature is operative; and he attains the highest development of his whole nature, only in the manifold relations of such society. There is a sense, indeed, in which the individual concedes something of personal liberty and advantage in exchange for the advantages which accrue to him from his social compact with his fellows. But there is a higher sense, in which every such concession not only secures a gain, but is in itself a gain, to the individual.[1] The obligation to society, then, is in the direction of the highest development of the individual; and the tendencies of individual progress are not towards the disintegration of civil society, but towards the better establishing and perfecting of it. Only let it be freely acknowledged, that the basis of civil society is a social compact between men acting as free, but social and moral, beings, and we reach the great conclusions, that all governments derive their just powers from the consent of the governed, and that civil society becomes

[1] Rousseau: Du Contrat social, pp. 6–8.

more and more authoritative in the true sense of that word, and more and more secure, as men advance in the development and appropriation of civil liberty.

We have seen that the controversy between the Realists and Nominalists led to the determination of the question which we have been considering. We need not be surprised at finding, however, that the relation of that contest to civil society was not apparent to the civilians and doctors of the Middle Ages, and that the theory of society to which it conducted was not formally defined till a comparatively recent date. For it has always been characteristic of political economists, that they attempt to adjust their theories to existing facts and received opinions; and, in doing this, their theories are frequently sacrificed. The existing facts of absolute government, both in Church and State, and the received opinions in regard to the irresponsible authority of such government, were too formidable to be attacked by the ecclesiastical philosophers of the Middle Ages, even in their speculations. And their speculations were largely influenced and modified, as well as arrested, by their philosophical traditions and their political and social environment. Hence it was reserved for a civilian and jurisconsult of the seventeenth century to be the first to apply the true principle of Nominalism in the domain of politics. To Hugo Grotius belongs the imperishable honor of having first defined the philosophic basis of civil society. In the prolegomena to his treatise, "De Jure Belli et Pacis," which he composed in 1625, he declared that the social impulse — "*societatis appetitus*" — is the foundation of life in communities, and that civil society is that state into which this impulse, acting freely and unselfishly, brings men together. It is significant that Aristotle had long before defined man as a "political animal,"[1] but he failed to work out the great thought which seems to have been present to his mind. He adopted the theory, that the family was the origin of the State, — a theory which led to conclusions which are quite inconsistent with the received data of political economy, and which has therefore been abandoned by all really thoughtful political philosophers.[2] We shall have occasion in the

[1] Aristotle: Politics, bk. i. chap. ii.
[2] Luthardt: Moral Truths of Christianity, p. 164. Locke: First Treatise of Government. Sir Henry Sumner Maine: Ancient Law, chap. v. pp. 162, 163.

next lecture to see how even this view was abandoned in the interest of a theocratic absolutism, which even the patriarchal idea of government was not adequate to justify. We shall also see how the operation of the great principle indicated by Christ was suspended for long centuries of imperial domination and ecclesiastical tyranny, so that it was not till after the Reformation that a Dutch civilian in exile at Paris formulated the true doctrine of civil liberty. Like all great thoughts, the thought of Grotius exhibited a marvellous fecundity. The English philosopher Hobbes, also sometime an exile like Grotius, seized the formula of the Dutch jurisconsult, and, under the influence of his eccentric genius, worked it out into the grotesque philosophy which has since been identified with his name.[1] Almost immediately Spinoza brought to bear upon the same subject the finer resources of his subtle speculation.[2] In England, Locke, Warburton, and Hoadley ranged themselves on the same side; while Sir Robert Filmer, and the political school which he founded, as earnestly contended against

---

[1] Hobbes: De Cive, and The Leviathan.
[2] Spinoza: Tractatus Theologico-politicus, chap. xvi.

the new doctrine, sometimes on the ground that the State had a patriarchal origin, sometimes on the theocratic postulate of the divine right of kings.[1] The most complete elaboration of the social-compact theory, however, was made by Rousseau in "Du Contrat social," published in 1761, in which he wrote what may be justly termed the first great philosophical treatise on civil society. His misguided genius, however, continually led him astray; and, through his eccentricities, the great principle of Grotius has been held responsible for conclusions not justly derivable from it. Perhaps it may be said, that the principle of Grotius, as perverted by Rousseau, led on to the French Revolution; while the same principle, as elaborated by Locke, Hoadley, and Warburton, has led on to the establishment on these shores of civil and religious liberty.

Let us now briefly indicate one or two conclusions from the foregoing considerations. The first of these is, that governments derive their just powers from the consent of the governed. So far as civil society is concerned, the will of the people is the supreme law. The doctrine of

[1] Sir Robert Filmer: Patriarcha.

a "higher law," then, has no place in a true philosophy of civil society. This doctrine, which has always been at once the plea of fanaticism and the last refuge of tyranny, is excluded from the domain of politics by the theory which is here propounded. Nevertheless, the true authority of government is distinctly guarded by the principle, that men, in forming and maintaining the social compact of civil society, are acting in obedience to impulses that must control them, and are moving towards the perfection of their being. It follows, then, that the power of government may be progressive along the line of social development, but that this progression must rest on the consent of the governed, and must be further controlled, not only by the will of the body politic, but also by the inalienable right which every soul has to the highest and best development of his own nature. There are, therefore, certain essential limitations to the power of government, which are interposed by the inalienable rights of man;[1] and there may be as many other limitations imposed as may be enacted by the popular will, provided such limitations do not work the destruction of civil society.

[1] John Stuart Mill: On Liberty.

Between the two extremes here indicated, there are certain debatable questions, such as the function of government in the matter of education and in the administration of charity. These are hereafter to be considered by us in connection with our principal topic, which is, The Relation of Christianity to Civil Society.

Before passing from this branch of our subject, let me make an appeal, — first, for the thoughtful consideration, and then for the hearty acceptance, of this theory of civil society; and this because I believe it to be the true theory, and because I believe it to be the theory on which all our own civil institutions are founded. Too often and too long have religious men maintained a certain reserve in acknowledging the correctness of the principle upon which the whole structure of our government rests. Because of this reserve, there is a widening breach between the teachers of religion and the leaders of political affairs. Religion is gravely suspected of being still identified with despotism, because religious teachers are supposed to be constantly appealing to a "higher law" in the domain of politics, and exhibiting a profound distrust in the principles of popular sovereignty.

It is one of the objects of these lectures, to indicate that popular sovereignty, organizing itself in civil society, and in obedience to the best and highest impulses of man's social and moral nature, is the legitimate outcome of the influence of Christianity, and that it is only under the social-compact theory, properly understood, that Christianity can freely act as the conservative of civil society.

Having now defined the philosophic basis of civil society, it only remains, that we should likewise define Christianity before we begin to consider the relation between them. The true theory of Christianity will be best considered in the next lecture, in the course of what I shall have to say of Jesus and his work. Let it suffice here to say, that the movement by which Christianity was formulated was, in a certain sense, the opposite of that which elaborated civil society. The latter began with the individual; that is, from below: the former began from above. The latter rests upon the consent of men : the former rests upon the command of God. The latter depends upon a social compact between equals : the former depends on loyalty to a personal law-giver and king. The State, or civil society, is not theocratic in any sense. The Church is theocratic, and is the only theocracy. This contradistinction constitutes the essential separateness of Church and State, and renders any attempt to unite, or combine, or formally to ally them, an embarrassment and a profound wrong to both. Uncombined and unallied, left free to act and re-act on each other, the relation between them may be mutually helpful. The moment constraint enters into this relation, it becomes hurtful. Here, then, are our two terms of relation, — a theocratic Church which is wholly non-political, and a social-compact State which is wholly secular. The bond that sustains the one is personal loyalty to a living, contemporary king and law-giver: the bond that sustains the other is the obligation that man, as a social and moral being, has to society. The authority upon which the one rests is the enactment and institution of a divine founder. The authority upon which the other rests is the will of the people. The point of contact between the two is the individual man. If man is a political being by nature, all his social and civil instincts are expanded, transformed, rectified, enlarged, by the influence of Christianity. Under its operation the *societatis appetitus* is transformed and expanded into brotherly love. The social compact is re-enforced by the characteristic Christian principle of the brotherhood of the human race. By Christianity a moral motive-power is supplied, which is far better than any mere pact or enactment in keeping society together; and that is, the charity that is not easily provoked, the love that works no ill to his neighbor. To the motives which tend to insure well-being in this world, it adds the loftier hopes, the nobler aspirations, the better purposes, that bind the Christian man to an endless future. It helps him to be a better citizen of this world, in teaching him that he has a citizenship in heaven. Christianity presides at the source and in the sanctuary of civil life. Through the individual conscience, the individual intelligence, the individual affections, — as these are the objects of divine grace, and then become the subjects of social and political power, — through these avenues, the living Christ is to-day operating upon civil society, and is showing himself more and more to be the Leader of civilization and the Ruler of the world.

LECTURE II.

THE ANSWER OF CHRIST, AND THE DEVELOPMENTS OF EUROPEAN HISTORY.

LECTURE II.

THE ANSWER OF CHRIST, AND THE DEVELOPMENTS OF EUROPEAN HISTORY.

"But Jesus perceived their wickedness, and said, Why tempt ye me, ye hypocrites? Shew me the tribute money. And they brought unto him a penny. And he saith unto them, Whose is this image and superscription? They say unto him, Cæsar's. Then saith he unto them, Render therefore unto Cæsar the things which are Cæsar's; and unto God the things that are God's." — ST. MATTHEW xxii. 18-21.

IT has already been pointed out, that the purpose of the Pharisees, in sending their disciples with the Herodians to Jesus, was, to betray him into one of two alternative dangers in defining his attitude towards the Roman civil authority. The craftiness with which their question was put was worthy of the deep-laid plan out of which it proceeded. The inquirers came to Jesus as to a Master in Israel, one who taught the way of God in truth, as though they would refer to him the settlement of a pending dispute. There was a subtle attempt at flattery, moreover, in their allusion to his conspicuous and manly independence, — his freedom from all kinds of social and political obsequiousness, — "Thou regardest not the person of men." They appealed to him, therefore, for an authoritative and out-spoken declaration, either for or against the lawfulness of a certain tribute, or tax, levied by Cæsar; believing that his answer, whether affirmative or negative, would serve their purpose of hostility to him. A brief consideration of the political and religious antagonisms of the time will show that their expectation was well founded. To the orthodox and patriotic Jews, the levying of this capitation-tax was doubly odious, not only as a burdensome exaction, but also as the badge of the subjection of the chosen people of God to a detested and despotic Gentile power. The religious and patriotic zeal of all the more respectable and devout was aroused into fierce opposition to this sacrilegious spoliation of the heritage of Jehovah. The coarse and brutal Roman procurator, whose office had special regard to the supervision of the revenue, had made this tax still more hateful by his contemptuous disdain of the scruples of the Jews. Of all the Jews, the Galileans were conspicuous for their patriotic opposition to the despotism under which the nation groaned; and it was not forgotten that Jesus belonged to Galilee. In the sacred precincts of the temple itself, within whose courts they were then standing, the Roman governor had not scrupled to slay Galilean worshippers, even at the foot of the altar, and to mingle their blood with the daily sacrifice. If, then, Jesus should answer affirmatively that it was lawful and right to pay this hated tribute, and so range himself on the side of the bloody tyrant, there would be an end of all his influence with his countrymen. Such an answer would, in their estimation, effectually dispose of all his pretensions to the Messiahship of the Jews. But if, on the other hand, he should declare, as a public and influential teacher, that it was not lawful and right to pay the tax, there were the Herodians ready to take the news of his treasonable utterance to the truculent Roman governor, who would surely make short work with any popular leader of whom they could say, "We have found him perverting the nation, and forbidding to give tribute to Cæsar."[1]

The exact position of the Herodians in regard

[1] St. Luke xxiii. 2.

to this and kindred subjects is involved in much obscurity. In attempting to ascertain their political opinions, we have little more than their name to guide us. This would seem to indicate, that as the partisans of Herod, who was an Idumæan in race, a Jew by conversion, and a satrap of the Roman emperor by appointment, they were the native upholders of the imperial authority, as represented by the petty prince from whom their name was derived. At all events, it is perfectly certain that they were ready to report any treasonable utterance of the Galilean Prophet to the Roman authorities. To such men it was sure to be both a congenial and a gainful vocation, to spy out treason, and hunt down the disaffected; and it was in order to this that they were now joined in ill-omened alliance with the Pharisees. The Herodians, then, are to be considered, whatever their own political and religious opinions, as the representatives on this occasion of that imperial policy to which it was supposed that the utterances of Jesus might be obnoxious, and to the resentment of which it was their purpose to betray him. Pontius Pilate, the vicegerent of such imperialism, was quartered at that moment in his official apartments in the palace of Herod. Within a few feet of where they stood were the stairs which connected the cloisters of the temple with the Tower of Antonia, from which the Roman guards overlooked the sacred enclosure. Jesus and his questioners were standing, then, within the very shadow, so to speak, of that overbearing and remorseless imperialism, which demanded, not only tribute, but homage, and even worship. For it must not be forgotten that the Roman theory of government was not less theocratic and exacting in its way than was the theory of the Jews. Though Rome, as a matter of wise policy, did not ordinarily interfere with the religions of conquered peoples, yet she always assumed the right to regulate them; and, even in enrolling them as *religiones licctæ*, she assumed and exercised what we would call a spiritual jurisdiction over the religions of the world. Nor was this all. The authority of the Roman State had always been supposed to rest on no popular right, but on a right assumed to be divine.[1] With Julius and Augustus Cæsar this theory was embodied in the cultus of the *imperium divum*. The poet Virgil

---

[1] James Bryce, D.C.L.: The Holy Roman Empire, p. 20.

taught the Roman world to salute the young Augustus as the divine boy who descended from the skies to institute on earth the reign of Jove.[1] From that time the person of the Cæsar was sacred. To him or to his Genius temples were erected, and divine honors paid, even while he was alive.[2] It soon came to be proclaimed, wherever the Roman eagles were displayed, that Cæsar was a god. In that weary and despairing age, amid the multitude of subjugated deities, the idea was not slow of acceptance, that there was one god, at least, whose power was no delusion, who could punish and reward, who could build up and destroy, — and that god was Cæsar. To acknowledge his divineness came to be the characteristic religion of the empire, and the worship of him was soon identified with loyalty. Victorious generals and imperial deputies, like the younger Pliny in a later age, made the yielding of divine honors to the emperor, the doing sacrifice to the statue of the Cæsar, a test, both of loyalty and of fitness to live.[3] There is strong ground for believ-

---

[1] Virgil: Georgics, i. 24; iv. 560.

[2] Bryce: The Holy Roman Empire, p. 23. Horace: Odes, iii. 3, 11. Ovid: Epistolarum ex Ponto, iv. 9, 105. Tacitus: Annales, i. 73; iii. 38.

[3] Robertson: History of the Christian Church, vol. i. p. 18.

ing that Pilate himself was prepared to impose this cult upon the subject-people over whom he was placed. When he removed his headquarters from Cæsarea to Jerusalem, he introduced the imperial standards bearing the image of the Cæsar into the Holy City; though he was compelled to do so by night, and in contemptuous defiance of the repeated and impassioned entreaties of the Jews. On another occasion he persisted in a similar policy in spite of tumult and insurrection, till an order from the emperor himself restrained the zeal of this too religious governor.[1] Upon the theory of Pilate, therefore, and of the Herodians, who on this occasion, at least, were the representatives of his opinions, the paying of tribute was due to Cæsar as an act of loyalty and homage, and as the acknowledgment of his divine authority. Because the Cæsar was divine, he was entitled to the allegiance and the tribute of all the peoples of the earth; and loyalty to Roman power meant the acknowledgment, not merely of the wisdom of Roman laws and the might of Roman arms, but the divineness of the imperial god.[2]

---

[1] Philo Judæus: Ad Caium, 30, 31, 45, 46.
[2] Bryce: Holy Roman Empire, pp. 5, 6.

With ready insight Jesus perceived the craftiness of his questioners, and the danger into which they would betray him. But, from his stand-point, the answer was obvious which would astonish and confound them. He called for the Roman coin in which the imperial tax was required to be paid. "Shew me the tribute money." They placed a Roman *denarius* in his hands. From coins of the same mintage still extant, we are able to understand the exact force of what he said. "On one side were stamped the haughty, beautiful features of the Emperor Tiberius, with all the wicked scorn upon the lip; on the obverse his title of *Pontifex Maximus*."[1] To the Pharisee, as I have said, the payment of this tribute was altogether odious, as the evidence of a political servitude which his soul abhorred; and the coin itself was to him an abominable thing, with an idolatrous image thereon, that suggested the pontifical supremacy of a Gentile despot, instead of the sole headship of Jehovah. To the Pharisee, therefore, this tribute was sacrilege. To the Roman, on the other hand, it was simple loyalty to one whose

---

[1] Canon Farrar: The Life of Christ, vol. ii. p. 231. Compare Bryce's Holy Roman Empire, p. 23.

power was irresistible because his authority was divine. The answer of Jesus, to the utter amazement of his questioners, took sides with neither of these alternative theories. He occupied a standpoint altogether different from theirs, — a standpoint not before occupied by any teacher. His answer, therefore, perplexed and confounded them; so that "they marvelled and left him, and went their way." To him the paying of this tribute was not at all what it seemed to either party of his questioners to be. In his estimation the *denarius* was simply the current coin of the realm, the symbol, both of commercial value, and of an acknowledged political and commercial obligation to contribute to the maintenance of the existing civil society, — nothing more. The fact that the coin was current, and had been struck at Cæsar's mint, was conclusive evidence that the imperial government was the acknowledged civil power. Give back, then, to Cæsar, he said, the tribute which the very currency of this coin proves that you have acknowledged yourselves bound to give, but render to God the things that are God's. And, saying this, he said implicitly to both Pharisee and Herodian, The payment of this tribute has not the significance that you attach to it, nor is civil society what you suppose it to be. Civil government is not theocratic in either the Jewish or the Roman sense, and the payment of a tax to it does not ascribe to it such a character. Religious scruples, then, and religious partisanship, have nothing to do with this matter. The payment of tribute to Cæsar is simply a political obligation, acknowledged to be binding by the very currency of this coin which you have received from his mint; but it is in no sense an act of religious homage. To give tribute to Cæsar is a duty, yes; but it is a political duty. Man's religious duty, the homage of his soul, is due only to his God.

It is evident, then, that Jesus occupied a new stand-point in politics, and defined a new relation between religion and civil society. It is important, therefore, that we should attentively consider what his point of view was, and by what steps he reached it, — all the more important, because, for reasons which are hereafter to be given, the position which he assumed was abandoned by his Church, and has yet to be regained in by far the greater part of Christendom. It must be obvious that nothing more than a mere outline-sketch can be here attempted of what has been termed the "plan" of Jesus; yet his plan is distinguished by such simplicity and consistency, and is so easily discernible in the authentic records of his earthly life and teaching, that a mere outline will suffice to define it. His plan, then, was to set up the kingdom of God in the world, of which kingdom he, as God, was to be the head and king; to establish the true theocracy, of which the elder theocracy of the Jews was but the type and preparation. He designed, moreover, that such theocracy should be wholly distinct from the kingdoms of this world. In a word, he decreed the total separation of Church and State; designing, that neither in alliance nor in antagonism, but through the conscience and the moral nature of the individual man, there should be established the only relation between Christianity and civil society.

Nothing is more certain than that Jesus assumed to be the Messiah of the Jews, the Prince of the house of David, whose mission was, to build up the long-expected kingdom of God. The prophetic announcement which proclaimed his coming was repeated in the first utterance of his own ministry, "The kingdom of God is at hand."

To the Jews this announcement seemed to have a definite meaning. It seemed to them to proclaim the immediate restoration of the old theocracy, the re-assertion of the autonomy of the chosen people, the throwing-off the yoke of a foreign oppressor, the restoration of royalty to the house of David. But Jesus intended both less and more: he intended, indeed, to set up the kingdom of God, and to assume, in virtue of his own divine royalty, the headship thereof; he intended to establish the true theocracy, which prophets had foretold; but, in order to this, he intended to separate his kingdom from every thing that was local, partial, preparatory; he intended to make it a universal and everlasting kingdom, belonging to both worlds, the seen and the unseen, to time and eternity; and therefore he intended to dissociate it from the kingdoms of this world.

It is not difficult to see in what respects the ideal of Jesus surpassed the elder theocracy, even in its best days. In accordance with the divine method, as revealed to us in all history, the elder dispensation was limited by the conditions of development and progress to which it was adjusted. The time had not yet come when the tribal instinct could be set aside. The most that could be done was, to expand it into the larger instinct of national life. Nor had the time yet come when the civil as distinguished from the ecclesiastical instinct could be altogether trusted to organize the people. Therefore the religious and ecclesiastical organization of Israel was made to take the place of civil society. With all its changes and modifications, however, it is evident that the elder dispensation was partly typical, partly special, and partly preparatory, and that it was not intended to be perpetuated in all its details in the new dispensation, which was to fulfil it. With divine insight, therefore, Jesus resolved to revive the theocracy in its ideal, that is to say, in its permanent and universal, form; and this involved the disconnecting of it, both in idea and form, from what was local, temporal, transitory.

The purpose, then, of Jesus, to establish a universal and everlasting kingdom, of which he himself, in virtue of his divine royalty, should be king, involved on his part the utter renunciation of all temporal and civil authority. It was not merely because he determined to found his kingdom on the law of self-sacrifice, and not on force, — to make love, and not coercion, its principle of cohesion, — that he renounced the temporal sovereignty of the kingdoms of this world; but it was also because the two kinds of sovereignty, the temporal and the spiritual, were incompatible, and could not be united without injury to both. The issue was distinctly presented to him in his temptation, and was then definitely settled. From the great decision which he then made, he never wavered. He saw, that for him, with his divine ideals and everlasting purpose, to undertake the headship of this world's kingdoms would be to renounce his divine mission. From the first, therefore, he never dallied with the thought of earthly sovereignty. Once, when called upon to exercise the judicial function, which the Jews naturally expected him, both as Messiah and Prophet, to undertake, he distinctly declined such a function, saying, "Man, who made me a judge or a divider over you?" So, on more than one occasion, he refused to exercise any of the official functions of civic life quite as persistently as he refused to appeal to force, or to lean on the sword of the military power. So also, and notably in our text, he referred the determination of the civic duty of his questioners to the terms of the social compact under which they lived, pointing to the mintage of the coin which they themselves had already accepted as current, to indicate the obligations of their political citizenship, and confining his own dogmatic utterance of what their duty was to the obligation which they owed, not to Cæsar, but to God. So, finally, when arraigned before Pilate on the charge of claiming to be a king, he solemnly reiterated the claim, but denied the accusation of his accusers by declaring that his "kingdom is not of this world." To the Roman such a claim was unintelligible. To his Jewish accusers, while it denied the charge which they formally made, it confessed the real grievance which they had against him. It was not that he claimed to be a king; it was not even that he claimed to be a king by divine right, and as the Son of God, that constituted the real fault which they found in him, — but it was because, while he claimed to be a king, he refused to exercise a temporal sovereignty. It was precisely because his kingdom was not of this world, and because he would not summon his servants to fight, and so to smite their heathen oppressors hip and thigh, that the Jews rejected his Messiahship, and delivered him up to die.

Reflection upon the nature of the kingdom which Jesus did set up, and upon the philosophical basis of civil society, confirms the view here taken of the essential incompatibility of ecclesiastical and civil power. From the point of view which we have already reached, it seems too evident to require further argument, that the Founder of Christianity designed that his Church should be forever separate from the civil State. The Church was instituted as a universal and enduring theocracy, of which Jesus himself was the head and king. Membership in his Church, he decreed, should depend on faith and grace, — faith in the recipient, and grace from himself, the giver, — and should consist in personal loyalty to himself as a living king, which loyalty was to be sustained, not only in the obedience of discipleship, but in personal communion with him in sacrament and prayer. This kingdom was to be fixed, unvarying, universal; having an "order" that could not be altered, and a "faith" that could not be changed: because such order was instituted by the Law-giver himself, who also delivered "the faith once for all" to his disciples. Civil society, on the other hand, was not instituted by the supreme Law-giver, nor was any institute of civil polity enacted by him. It is not pretended by any that the Founder of Christianity undertook in any sense to constitute a State, though undoubtedly he did constitute a Church. While, therefore, the basis of Christianity is altogether theocratic, the only philosophical basis of civil society is found, in the absence of any enactment and institution thereof, to be a social compact between individual men, acting in accordance with the moral and social impulses of their nature. The very fact, then, that Jesus did constitute his Church, making it theocratic, but did not constitute the State, leaving it to be organized or elaborated by the impulses towards society, which already existed in human nature, is in itself conclusive proof, that, in his design, the Church was to be distinct and separate from the civil power.

But the argument can be pushed a step farther. It is to be observed, that, while Jesus designed that his kingdom should not interfere with the functions of civil society, he not only refrained from recognizing the State as a corresponding theocracy, but he designed that the old claim of divine right or theocratic authority on the part of the State should be eventually overthrown, and that civil society should rest on a secular and social compact between men as men. It is not more certain that he intended that the Church should be a theocracy than that he intended that the State should rest its claim to authority simply on the consent of the governed: but, in the case of the Church, he enacted his purpose in its very constitution; while, in the case of the State, he simply set a principle in operation that would eventually work out his design. While Jesus, in establishing his kingdom in virtue of his own divine royalty, demanded the allegiance and loyalty of his disciples, yet, in the very act of doing this of divine right, he inaugurated a principle that would eventually make a similar claim on the part of any earthly kingdom impossible. For in making personal repentance, personal faith, and the gift of personal grace, the condition of membership in his kingdom, he emancipated the individual man, and declared the individual, and not the tribe, the nation, or the race, to be the ethical

subject. Before that time, at least among the
Gentile nations, the individual man had been as
nothing. Under the old theory of government, he
had simply been an undivided and unconsidered
part of the State. His dignity, if any he had, was
measured by the accident of birth, or of wealth, or
of achievement. All except the few so distinguished were the "*profanum vulgus*," without individuality and without rights. Nothing in all
history is so pathetic as the unlegendary insig-
nificance of the masses of mankind at the beginning of the Christian era. When to the burden
of external oppression we add the consideration of
the dumb, hopeless misery which belonged to the
complete obliteration of all individuality, the utter
extermination of all personal dignity and self-respect wrought by the civil and military tyrannies
of that time, we gain an idea, not otherwise at-
tainable, of the utter wretchedness of that ancient
world. In such a state of things, the acceptance
of Christianity was a wakening from the dead, —
a personal emancipation. By it, for the first time
in long, dreary ages, the masses of mankind were
individualized. The first startling note of the
gospel, in convicting the hearer of sin, awakened

in him, for the first time perhaps, the sense of individual responsibility: and with the sense of pardon came the sublime sense of sonship to quicken and crown his wondering soul; for it was the distinguishing peculiarity of Christianity, that it dealt, not with men in the mass, but with men as individuals. It taught the great truth, that the individual alone is the ethical subject. It denounced its penalties, and promised its gracious rewards to the individual soul; and, in thus resolving humanity into individuals, it set in motion a principle which was sure eventually to work man's political emancipation. It is impossible to exaggerate — it is often difficult for us to understand — the elevating force of the gospel when it was first preached in the Roman empire. The poor, the outcast, the oppressed, became conscious of a dignity and a self-determining power that made their life, even in this world, altogether different from what it before had been. He who had won citizenship in the kingdom of God could not be in real subjection to any man. Constantly, therefore, and silently, the gospel in the apostolic age was working emancipation, and was undermining the old basis of authority on which the despotism of the Roman Government rested. And herein arose a danger to Christianity itself, that the apostles were not slow to discover, and to warn the faithful against. The emancipation of the Christian was not intended to be a violent one. In no case was it intended to work or encourage social or political insubordination. It was not designed to discredit government or social order. Nay, it was not designed to deny, but rather to insist upon, the divine sanction of all such governments as should be actually established until better should be compassed in the natural and regular way. Even heathen governments were of divine sanction, not in the sense of having been instituted by God, but in the sense of resting for their true authority upon a compact or consent which was the outcome of social impulses implanted by God in human nature, and of serving purposes approved by God; and the apostolic injunction was, therefore, both timely and right, that "every soul should be subject unto the higher powers. For there is no power but of God: the powers that be are ordained of God."[1] "Wherefore ye must needs be subject, not only for wrath, but also

[1] Romans xiii. 1.

for conscience sake."[1] The emancipation offered by the gospel, then, was perfectly compatible with obedience to constituted authority. It was far more complete and profound than any that mere insubordination or revolution could effect. It completely changed the recognized basis of authority in civil society. It revealed to man, that civil government rested on no higher authority than the individual consent and the individual conscience, and that these are a sufficient basis for it to rest on; and that, in being subject for conscience' sake, man could still be free under any civil goverment, ay, even in bonds, if, as a matter of conscience and of his own free will, he should consent to be in subjection.

Here, then, was the relation established by Christ between Christianity and civil society. The Church was a pure theocracy, with a fixed faith and order, and ruled over by a living king. Under this theocracy, men were emancipated into the freedom, the dignity, the responsibility, of individuality. From this new stand-point, civil society was seen to be wholly distinct from the Church, and to have no other basis than the con-

[1] Romans xiii. 5.

sent of the people. Nevertheless, to yield that consent was an obligation of conscience, since civil society is in accordance with man's nature and God's will; and therefore "the powers that be are ordained of God." Under the relation so established, the Church was left free, notwithstanding her fixed order, to adjust her organization, so to speak, to external conditions.[1] So could she enter into such relations with any State as would range her on the side of the peace and well-being of society. The very distinction so plainly worked out in Church history between the Church's fixed order and variable organization clearly indicates, that, while the one was divinely appointed, the other was of human origin and authority; and the actual attitude assumed and maintained by the Church in the apostolic and subapostolic age is perfectly consistent therewith. For more than two centuries the Church undertook to exercise no temporal authority, and sought no recognition from, or alliance with, the civil power. And this was not at all because the State

[1] I trust I may refer without impropriety to a sermon on the Polity of the Church, preached by me before the Clerical Association of Cleveland in 1880, and published, in which the distinction between "order" and "organization" is pointed out.

was heathen; for the apostolic teaching was, that even a heathen government had the divine sanction, as we have seen: but it was because the attitude and relation instituted by Christ were not forgotten or departed from in the Church's early and most triumphant days. Nevertheless, the time did come when this relation and this attitude were abandoned. In an evil hour the Church yielded to the patronage of an unbaptized emperor,[1] and submitted to an alliance with the powers of this world. Then it was that the Church of Christ consented to become, in some respects at least, a department of the civil power. From that moment her true glory began to be obscured, her triumphs to be limited, and the unnumbered evils of Byzantinism and the Papacy, and of the contest between them, to afflict the Christian world, and to retard the civilization and evangelization of the human race.

In order to understand the full import of this disastrous alliance, which an eminent Christian historian has fitly termed "one of the greatest *tours d'addresse* that Satan ever played,"[2] it will

---

[1] It is noteworthy that Constantine was not baptized till just before his death.   [2] Arnold: Miscellaneous Works, p. 436.

be necessary to consider for a moment what authority Constantine claimed as emperor, how far his pretensions were renounced or modified in nominally embracing Christianity, and to what extent he imposed his pretensions on the Church. Let it be remembered, then, that, as emperor, Constantine, and all his imperial predecessors, had based their authority on a divine right to rule. From the time of Augustus Cæsar the emperors were acknowledged as vicegerents of God. "Their persons were hallowed by the office of *Pontifex Maximus* and the tribunitian power."[1] Poets, as has been already pointed out, had sung the advent of the young Augustus as the descent of a divine boy from the skies, who should deliver and bless mankind. "The effigy of the emperors was sacred, even on a coin."[2] "Divine honors were paid to them in life as well as after death."[3] "In the confused multiplicity of mythologies, the worship of the emperor was the only worship common to the whole Roman world."[4] Now, when Constantine accepted Christianity, some of these pretensions were modified certainly; but none of them were wholly renounced. "Under

[1] Bryce: Holy Roman Empire, p. 23. [2] Ibid. [3] Ibid. [4] Ibid.

the new religion the form of adoration vanished: the sentiment of reverence remained."[1] The title and office of *Pontifex Maximus* were retained, and adapted to the new condition of affairs. The right to control the Church as well as the State was promptly asserted, and was formally admitted at Nicæa and elsewhere by a too subservient hierarchy.[2] Eusebius speaks of Constantine as a kind of general bishop,[3] and relates, that, on one occasion, the emperor told some episcopal guests, that, as they were bishops within the Church, so God had made him bishop without it.[4] And in numberless ways he proceeded to lord it over Christ's heritage, placing himself at the head of the Church, and subordinating the spiritual to the civil power.

Apart from the secularization of the Church and the depravation of Christianity which resulted from this unholy alliance, important consequences of another kind, and equally disastrous, began to flow from it. The clergy, leaning on the secular arm, and defending the emperor's assumptions of

---

[1] Bryce: Holy Roman Empire, p. 23.   [2] Ibid.
[3] Robertson: History of the Christian Church, vol. i. p. 419.
[4] Ibid. 421.

power, soon began to formulate the idea of a universal or world-church, to correspond exactly with the empire or world-state. As the empire, ordained of God, was one; so should the Church's unity be a like imperial unity. St. Augustine, in his great work, "The City of God," worked out a portion of this ideal relation. The further thought soon followed of a world-bishop or Pope, to correspond with the world-king or emperor; and this was the genesis of the Papacy.[1] Circumstances favored the complete development of the idea. The removal of the seat of empire from old Rome to "New Rome," or Constantinople, universalized the civil idea, but correspondingly weakened it. The irruption of the barbarians, who found nothing to respect, and spared nothing, in the West but the power of the Roman see; the division of the empire, and the growing influence of the bishops of Rome in that time of tumult, — continued to exalt the ecclesiastical power of the Popes, till at length, in the pretensions of Hadrian I.,[2] the spiritual supremacy of the successor of Peter was proclaimed: and when Leo

---

[1] Bryce: Holy Roman Empire, p. 91 *et seq.*
[2] Abbé Guettée: The Papacy, p. 258.

III. placed the iron crown on the brow of Charlemagne, the temporal supremacy of the Papal see seemed also to be acknowledged, at least in the West. The time speedily came when the Papal pretensions became quite unendurable by the emperor. It is still a question as to how far Charlemagne intended, by receiving his crown at the Pope's hands, to acknowledge the Pope's superior authority. Certain it is, that the story, so long believed, that Constantine had, by special grant, invested Pope Sylvester with imperial authority in the West, and that it was on that account that Charlemagne knelt to receive the iron crown, is false. But at all events, from that time on, in spite of occasional conflicts, the twofold idea of a world-monarchy and a world-church yielded support to both Papal and imperial despotism, till the subjugation of Christendom seemed to be complete. Nor did philosophy fail to lend its aid to this disastrous alliance. The influence of Realism in establishing a philosophical basis for absolutism, both in Church and State, has already been pointed out.[1] Under the influence of that philosophy, the individual was once more obliter-

---

[1] Lecture i.; also Holy Roman Empire, p. 97.

ated in religion and society. The despotic idea of the State was re-established, and at the same time the true idea of the Church as a divine theocracy was overthrown. By a perfectly logical retribution, the Church, in grasping at temporal authority, lost its true spiritual power, and, in seizing the kingdom of this world, placed itself in a position to be eventually enslaved by it. Meanwhile the history of mediæval European civilization was the record of much good commingled with no little evil; and of the evil it is not too much to say, that most of it is directly attributable to the alliance of Church and State.

Our present purpose requires us, however, to devote our attention chiefly to the development of the relation between Church and State in English history. Our limits will not permit us to study the many vicissitudes through which that relation passed under British, Saxon, and Danish princes, and under Plantagenet and Tudor kings. Nor can we consider the many questions, doctrinal and ecclesiastical, which were settled or unsettled at the time of the English Reformation, further than as these have immediate bearing upon the relation between the Church and the civil authority. It must suffice for us to point out, that while the English Church did reform its doctrines, and regain its ecclesiastical independence of the Papal despotism, it did not rescue itself from the tyranny of the civil power. Circumstances had all along been favorable to the maintenance of a close alliance between Church and State. In the long contest between the English Church and the Papacy, the State had usually been the bulwark of the Church against Papal aggression. In Magna Charta, in the Constitutions of Clarendon, in the Statute of *Præmunire*, the secular arm had undoubtedly been outstretched to defend the Church as well as the State against a foreign spiritual despotism. It was natural, therefore, at the Reformation, that the relations between Church and State should be made more intimate, and should exalt, rather than detract from, the sovereignty of the civil power. Accordingly, we find, that, when Henry VIII. claimed for himself a supremacy in matters ecclesiastical which equalled the supremacy claimed and exercised by Constantine, the Church made but feeble resistance. The doctrine of the royal supremacy was pushed to its greatest extreme; and the assumptions of the crown, after a verbal modification, were yielded to.[1] Though this doctrine was somewhat softened, it was not really modified, in the reigns of Edward, Elizabeth, James, and Charles. Under its provisions the free Church of England, autonomous, apostolic, historic, reformed, consented to become a "Church established by law;" to become, in some respects, a department of State; to be used for political purposes; to become the apologist and defender of political measures; in a word, to do duty as an "Establishment:" and it is out of this unfortunate relation that most of the evils that have since afflicted the English Church have proceeded.

Resistance to such an arrangement was inevitable. Unfortunately, this resistance was allowed to organize itself outside of the Church instead of within it, and to become a movement hostile to the Church's order. Time does not permit us to do more than summarize the characteristics of the great Puritan re-action. Undoubtedly, it had its origin partly in doctrinal divergences; and it

---

[1] Blunt: Reformation in England, pp. 111-134. Hardwick: History of the Christian Church during the Reformation, pp. 191-193. Burnet: History of the Reformation, vol. i. pp. 112, 113.

assumed a certain doctrinal type, with which at present we have nothing to do. It is also undeniable, that it finally antagonized itself against the Church's order as well as against its organization. But no candid examination of the origin and progress of Puritanism can escape the conclusion, that the whole movement, including Independency, was mainly political, and was directed against certain evils that were attributed to the Establishment and to the doctrine of royal supremacy. The majority of the Elizabethan, Jacobean, and early Caroline bishops consented to become the champions of the royal prerogative, of the doctrine of non-resistance, and of the divine right of kings.[1] The supreme questions on which the Puritans and Independents antagonized the Church were political, and not religious.[2] James I. declared in Parliament, that it was not on religious, but on political, grounds that the Puritans differed from himself and his supporters;[3] and Cromwell distinctly and repeatedly declared in 1653, that the origin of the war was not religious.[4] The undiscriminating

---

[1] Arnold: Lectures on Modern History, p. 232.   [2] Ibid.
[3] Speech of James I. in Parliamentary History, vol. i. p. 982.
[4] Carlyle: Cromwell, vol. iii. p. 103.

espousal of the royal cause, with all its dangerous political and ecclesiastical pretensions, by Laud, and the rest of the hierarchy under Charles I., alienated large numbers of the people; so that it may be said, that it was not against the Church, but against the Establishment, that the great Revolution directed its blind and iconoclastic fury. We shall hereafter have occasion to remark how Laud's zeal, not for the Church, but for the Establishment, drove out many of the Church's children, some of whom came to America, and here essayed to establish a system that should be free from the evils inflicted by the archbishop's heavy hand. For the present it is enough to point out, that, in all those troublesome times, the Church was fighting battles not her own, and that the many evils of dissent and nonconformity by which she was so sore bestead were but the fruits of the unhappy alliance which she made with the kingdom of this world.

It must not be forgotten, however, that, while the Puritans arrayed themselves against the Establishment, it was not because they objected to the alliance or union of Church and State, but it was because they opposed the terms of the existing alliance. They objected with good reason to the supremacy of the State over the Church; but they desired to establish the opposite, and quite as objectionable, extreme, in making the Church supreme over the State. In other words, they desired that the State should be administered on religious principles, and that they should define and apply those principles, — a theory of civil and religious liberty that has not yet perished from the face of the earth. It is a noteworthy fact, that the Puritans would have remained in the Church on these terms, only stipulating that the hierarchy should be composed of Puritan bishops, and that the State should be subservient to them. For a long time it was the theory of the Puritans, that the civil power could be so reformed as to become a willing instrument in the hands of the "saints." But at length many of the stronger spirits among them grew weary of waiting for such an adjustment, and went off into the peculiar separatism called Independency. Subsequently many of the remaining Puritans became Presbyterians, because the bishops of the Church refused to accept their peculiar theocratic views; and then the Church was assailed on both sides, because of her alliance with the State. Circumstances, combined with the greater simplicity and consistency of their early political opinions, soon gave the predominance of power to the Independents; but it was yet too soon for any party to become the consistent advocates of a total separation of Church and State. When the Independents came into power, they soon developed a more bigoted and intolerant theory of theocratic government than the early Puritans. Cromwell seized the reins of power as the Lord's anointed, and based his claim to authority, not on the will of the people, but on the will of God. He united in his own person the office of civil and military dictator, of Pope, of emperor, and of *Pontifex Maximus*, and undertook to rule the consciences of men with quite as firm a hand as he ruled their conduct.[1] Indeed, so odious did this tyranny become, in matters both civil and religious, that it soon became apparent that the old Establishment was better than the new theocracy;[2] and the Presbyterians united with Churchmen, and all the sincerest friends of liberty throughout the realm, in bringing back the exiled Stuarts to the English throne.

[1] Carlyle: Cromwell, vol. iii. 105 *et seq.*
[2] Hume: History of England, vol. vii. pp. 258–308.

The Revolution of 1688, and the subsequent settlement of the Hanoverian succession, developed yet another stage in the adjustment of the relation between Church and State. At the Restoration the old doctrines of non-resistance, of the royal supremacy, and of the divine right of kings, re-appeared with increased vigor; and, as was natural, the clergy, and especially the bishops, became the defenders of them. It was indeed quite natural that the hierarchy that had suffered and gone into exile with the house of Stuart, and now had been restored with the king, should identify the rights and authority of the Church with the royal cause, and refuse to distinguish between loyalty to the Church and loyalty to the king. Accordingly, when, after the Revolution of 1688, it became necessary to take the oaths to William and Mary, and to renounce the house of Stuart, five bishops, including the primate, submitted to deprivation rather than make the distinction. The vacant sees were at once filled with prelates who took a more liberal, and, as we can see, a more just and sound, view of the matter. With the surrender of the old doctrine of divine right, on which the claims of the house of Stuart rested, it became necessary to establish a new doctrine of the true basis of civil society. This was undertaken by Locke,[1] who was followed by Hoadley[2] and Warburton,[3] who elaborated with great learning what is called the social-compact theory of government, — a theory, which, it is not too much to say, embodied the principles long before set in operation by the gospel of Christ, registered the results of the Nominalistic philosophy, and led on to the establishment on these shores of civil liberty.[4] Unhappily, however, the great and philosophical thinkers who did this service for the State, were not free to plead for the Church's liberty also. The burden of the Establishment still weighed down the Church's life.[5] The concordat between Church and State was undisturbed, and still remains in force;[6] and later English writers and thinkers, who were well

---

[1] Locke: Of Government, and Of Civil Government.

[2] Bishop Hoadley: The Original and Institution of Civil Government.

[3] Bishop Warburton: The Alliance between Church and State, bk i.

[4] The reader is referred to the admirable notes of Bishop Whittingham to Palmer's Treatise on the Church, vol. ii. pp. 291-342.

[5] See the works of Locke, Hoadley, and Warburton, above referred to.

[6] For an accurate statement of the terms of the actual existing concordat between Church and State in England, see an able article in the British Critic for April, 1839, art. iii. pp. 321-367.

qualified by their correct views, both of civil society and of the Church's historic and theocratic constitution, to take the only consistent view of the relation between them, have been limited by the condition of being required to defend the Establishment, either on principle or from expediency.[1] For this reason the true relation between Christianity and civil society — as to be seen only from the Churchman's stand-point — has yet to be defined in English Christian literature. I believe that more auspicious conditions surround our inquiry, and that on these shores, and for the first time in centuries of political and ecclesiastical strife, there is room and opportunity for true Christian statesmanship. I also venture to believe, that such statesmanship must sooner or later occupy the point of view of the American Churchman, who, while he holds that the Church is a theocracy, also holds that the State is merely a secular and social compact, though not the less authoritative for that reason; and who believes that we, in this land, are in a

---

[1] See Mr. Gladstone's The State in its Relations with the Church, chap. iv. Also Bishop Warburton's Alliance between Church and State, part ii. sect. iii.

condition freely to realize the relation between Christianity and civil society indicated by Christ himself, when he uttered the words so often and so long misunderstood, "Render unto Cæsar the things which are Cæsar's, and unto God the things that are God's."

LECTURE III.

THE ANSWER OF CHRIST, AND THE DEVELOPMENTS OF AMERICAN HISTORY.

LECTURE III.

THE ANSWER OF CHRIST, AND THE DEVELOPMENTS OF AMERICAN HISTORY.

"If thou let this man go, thou art not Cæsar's friend." — ST. JOHN xix. 12.

THE charge which the Jews preferred against Jesus — that, in making himself a king, he put himself and his kingdom into opposition to the Cæsar and his imperial power — was both false and true. It was false in the sense in which the Jews intended it. It was true in a deeper sense than they or Pilate could understand. Jesus had already completely renounced all claim to sovereignty over the kingdoms of this world; and it was the capital fault which the Jews found in him, that he had made and persisted in such renunciation. Not only so, but with equal persistency he had refused, both to ally himself with and to antagonize the civil power, upon the ground so little understood in that day and since, that his "kingdom is not of this world." The conspicuous indifference of Jesus to temporal honors, and his utter refusal of temporal authority, even when his countrymen were eager to thrust it upon him, were sufficient evidence of the falseness and malignity of the charge that was made against him. Nevertheless, it was true that there was an irreconcilable antagonism between the theocratic imperialism of the Cæsar and the gospel of the kingdom of God. In that gospel a principle was set in operation among men, that was sure, sooner or later, to work human emancipation. It was a principle, that in individualizing man, in awaking him to a realizing sense of his personal dignity and personal responsibility, and in raising him by faith and through grace "into the glorious liberty of the children of God," was, sooner or later, to render all human tyrannies utterly intolerable, — a principle which, unless the Church had unworthily consented in a woful after-time to surrender it, would long since have banished Cæsarism, with its preposterous claim of divine right, from the face of the earth. There was a profound and irreconcilable issue, then, between Christianity and the theocratic imperialism of the Cæsar; but it was not to be settled in Pilate's judgment-hall: nor did Pilate, or the noisy mob who clamored before the *prætorium* for the "innocent blood," understand that issue at all. It was not to be settled by condemning Jesus the king, nor by smiting him to death. It was not to be settled by the stroke of fiery persecutions, nor by the oppositions of either superstition or philosophy. It was not to be settled by the surrender of the Christian Church to the same haughty and theocratic imperialism in the person of Constantine, emperor and "*Pontifex Maximus.*" It was not to be settled by the establishment of the daring claim of the Papacy to supreme temporal and spiritual power. It was not to be settled by the resumption in England of imperial supremacy over the Church by English kings. It was not to be settled by the erection of the revolutionary theocracy of the Commonwealth upon the ruins of such supremacy. It was not to be settled in any alliance between Church and State, any more than in the triumph of either over the other; but it was to be settled in the adjustment finally to be made between membership and discipleship in a purely spiritual and theocratic kingdom on the one hand,

and citizenship in a purely secular and civil society on the other.

I need not recapitulate what has been said already of the evils which resulted from the Church's surrender to Constantine, and from the subsequent development of Byzantinism and the Papacy. From the last of these the English Church was happily freed at the Reformation, but it was not her happiness then to escape from the tyranny of the temporal power. Indeed, under the virtual concordat then and subsequently forced upon her, she has been compelled to do duty as an Establishment, and too often to become the instrument of, and the apologist for, the arbitrary and tyrannical exercise of the civil authority. The peculiar calamity of this most unhappy conjunction cannot be exaggerated. For centuries the English Church has occupied a false position, and has been held responsible for the very oppression of which she herself has been the worst victim. It is difficult for an American Churchman to repress a feeling of sorrowful indignation when he remembers how our mother Church has been used by many a despotic cabal under Tudor and Stuart and Hanoverian, by Whig and Tory administrations, by secularist and infidel ministries, to serve ends utterly alien to her true polity, and to further purposes, which, if her true voice could have been heard, she would have renounced as utterly unworthy. It is a truth which cannot, I believe, be too much insisted on, that almost all the evils which have afflicted and still afflict English Christianity have been caused or provoked by the burden of the royal supremacy which the English Church has had thrust upon her. In consenting to do duty as a Church established by law, she has apparently identified herself and her fortunes with a merely human power. It was against this arrangement, and the policy which resulted from it, and not necessarily against the Church as Christ's kingdom, that English nonconformity was first arrayed, until such nonconformity was in some instances driven out by the secular arm, and made strong and formidable by persecution. So calamitous was this ill-omened alliance, that the revolution which first hurled the Stuart dynasty from the throne dragged the Church down with it; and it was not till the Stuarts were finally banished from the kingdom, that the Church was delivered from the task, long so servilely performed, of defending the divine right of kings. With the accession of William and Mary, the Church was free and prompt to assume a truer relation to the State; and it will remain an imperishable honor to the English Church, that some of her bishops were among the first to enunciate formally the great truth, that the authority of civil government is derived solely from the consent of the governed, and so to lay down the true basis of civil society.[1] But, in the mean time, even before the Church was free to formulate this principle, her children were engaged, beneath other skies, in its practical realization. Meantime a great movement was begun out of England toward a vast continent, which for long centuries had been hidden in the West, as if reserved to be the forum in which all the questions which had hitherto vexed the world should find their final adjudication. Hither the sons of English Christianity came to work out, for the most part unconsciously, and even in spite of their own obstructive methods, the great experiment of human liberty. And here, under these open heavens, I believe the world is destined to witness for the first time in history

[1] Hoadley and Warburton.

the establishment of the true relation between Christianity and civil society.

A brief consideration, then, of some of the most important influences that were active in shaping the beginnings of our national life, will be indispensable to our present purpose. And the first remark that I make in this connection is, that the impulse which began, and in large measure accomplished, the colonization of our territory, was mainly commercial, and not political or religious. The age of the Reformation was distinguished by a great outburst of energy, which signalized itself, under Henry VIII., Elizabeth, and James I., in maritime adventure, commercial enterprise, and especially in those great colonizing movements which attested the restlessness of the age and the vigor of the English people. The earliest attempts at American colonization had no connection whatever with political or religious discontent. When we remember that Virginia, the Carolinas, Georgia, and New York were settled wholly in obedience to this commercial and colonizing instinct, it will be seen how groundless is the claim, that the beginnings of our national life were due to political or religious grievances in the mother country. When it is observed, moreover, that the colonies, like Virginia and the Carolinas, which confessedly were not planted by religious or political propagandism, were at least as forward in the development and establishment of civil and religious liberty as were those, like Massachusetts and Connecticut, which were settled from alleged religious and political motives, we see reason for concluding that the direction and development of our national life towards the realization of liberty were shaped and determined, not so much by the original impulses which drove the colonists hither, or by any of them, as by the peculiar circumstances which taught independence and self-reliance to all the colonists alike. No doubt, there were Puritan colonies and Quaker plantations and Lutheran settlements: but, then, there were Church-of-England colonies also; and when we find a Church-of-England colony, like Virginia for instance, actually leading in the race and in the fight for freedom, and that, too, from the very beginning, it will not do to say that any separatist religious impulse, like Puritanism or Independency for instance, was the sole source, or even a distinguishing source, from which our liberties have

sprung. Nay,—for our argument is cumulative,
—the very fact that anti-Puritan Virginia did actually outstrip Puritan Massachusetts in the race for liberty, as we shall have occasion to notice presently, suggests the fact, which is otherwise verifiable, that it was not because of Puritanism, but rather in spite of it,' that our liberties were achieved at last. And the same is true of each of the characteristic religious movements of the period. If Puritanism had succeeded in carrying out its plans, we should have had no civil or religious liberty at all; but we should have had a pure theocracy of the most despotic type, in which the "saints," led by their ministers, would have ruled with iron hand the temporal and spiritual affairs of the commonwealth. If the Quaker idea had prevailed, we should have had religious toleration indeed of every thing but a Church; since the tendencies of Quakerism would have abolished the Church altogether, and made the State take its place. If the Establishment idea had prevailed, we should have had such an alliance of Church and State as still exists in England. But neither of these ideas prevailed. The movement towards civil and religious liberty was due to none of

them, but was rather due to the removal of factitious restraint and traditional hinderances from all the colonists alike; to the throwing of them alike upon the responsibilities of Christian manhood, and the leaving of them free, as men, to yield to the impulses which move Christian men to organize civil society.

The simple truth is, that the very emigration of the colonists was their emancipation. No matter what impulse drove them forth from the mother-land, it exiled them into liberty; and the broad Atlantic kept watch and ward over them while they realized and appropriated their liberty in the institutions of a free State. An examination of the early history of all the colonies will disclose the fact, that each one of them was practically free, almost from the very beginning, to frame its own government, and to make that government representative of and responsible to the people. More than a year before the Pilgrims landed at Plymouth, the colonists of Virginia had actually organized a government which was practically as free, and as responsible to themselves, as was the government provided for by the famous covenant drawn up in the cabin of "The Mayflower."[1] And so it will be seen, that just as fast as the settlers on these shores realized their independence, and their need of self-reliance and of the mutual protection of social order, they proceeded to organize civil society for themselves, as a social compact, and as deriving its authority really from the consent of the governed. Though attempts were made in the first instance to impose institutions upon the colonists from the mother-land, as, for instance, in the earlier proprietary charters, and in the famous plan of government drawn up for South Carolina by Locke and Shaftesbury; yet in every case those cumbersome and useless forms were speedily outgrown and swept aside, and the people were practically left free to organize society for themselves. The colonists were in a manner forced to realize their individuality, with the sense of personal dignity and personal responsibility belonging to it; and they were moved to organize self-government, both by the dangers and necessities which pressed upon them from without, and by the social and

---

[1] Bancroft: History of the United States, vol. i. pp. 118, 119. It is to be noted, that the references to Bancroft's History are all made to the edition of 1879, Little, Brown, & Co., Boston.

civil instinct which impelled them from within. Such hinderances as were interposed by proprietary councils and colonial governors were quietly ignored or forcibly put aside, and the more intimate and formidable hinderances of traditional opinion were quietly outgrown. With occasional disturbances and retrogressions, but with general and remarkable vigor, the colonists moved on towards the fuller and more complete realization of popular government. For the first time in the world's history the august spectacle was seen of free and equal men acting in accordance with their own social and civil instincts, and organizing free and responsible civil society, the sanction and authority of which were to rest wholly on their own consent. And the interest and dignity of this great movement are only enhanced by the fact, that, for the most part, it was engaged in almost unconsciously by the actors themselves. It is not too much to say, that the colonists grew into freedom, and, all along, were building wiser than they knew. It has been well said, that the New-England colonists came over to build a Zion, and to this end they directed all their conscious efforts; but all the while it was not a Zion, but a

State, that they were building.[1] So in Massachusetts and Virginia, in Connecticut and Carolina, in New York and Pennsylvania, the colonists were led, not by their conscious ideals, but often in spite of them, to build a great government of the people, by the people, and for the people, to be a home for the aspiring and a refuge for the oppressed of the human race. It is a salutary corrective of much that we have been hearing for many years past, to remember, that it was not in Puritan New England, but in cavalier Virginia, that the plant of liberty grew most rapidly, and soonest bore its ripened fruit. It was George Mason, the stanch and devout Virginia Churchman, who drew up the Declaration of Rights that was subsequently embodied, but not improved or enlarged, in the Declaration of Independence; and Mason's Declaration was unanimously adopted by the Virginia colonial legislature, a vast majority of whom were Churchmen. And not only was this the first and most notable declaration of civil liberty, but it was the very first declaration of religious liberty as well: for, scores of years before the laws of religious intolerance were ex-

[1] Lowell: New England Two Centuries Ago, p. 238.

punged from the statute-books of Massachusetts and Connecticut, the Virginia House of Burgesses declared in this immortal document, that "Religion can be directed only by reason and conviction, and not by force and violence; and therefore all men are equally entitled to the free exercise of it according to the dictates of conscience; and it is the mutual duty of all to practise Christian forbearance, love, and charity towards each other."[1]

The achievement of religious liberty, indeed, was a far more difficult and complicated task than the accomplishment of civil freedom. In order to understand it, we must consider briefly the three principal schools of religious thought which conditioned the problem in the different colonies. These were Puritanism, Quakerism, and Anglicanism; meaning by the last, that relation to the Establishment which was sustained by all Churchmen in colonial times. Let us consider these in the order named.

We have seen that Puritanism, as it developed itself in England under Elizabeth and James, was formally theological and philosophical, but was

[1] Bancroft: History of the United States, vol. v. pp. 260-262.

really political. In its own consciousness, however, it was altogether religious, and took on the type, as it advanced, of a stern and gloomy fanaticism. With its theological opinions and religious character we have here nothing to do, except as these affected its relations to the State or civil society. The mass of the Puritans were not originally opposed to the hierarchy. Indeed, several of the bishops themselves belonged to the Puritan party. Nor were the Puritans opposed to the alliance of Church and State. They only insisted on inverting the terms of that alliance so as to make the State entirely subservient to the Church. Their complaint was, that the civil power would not carry the Reformation to the lengths which they desired; and for a long time their hope was, that the State might be reduced to such subjection to them as to become obedient to their wishes. A few of the most earnest and devout soon relinquished this hope, and became separatists under the name of Independents. These, in theory at least, soon began to call for the abrogation of the Establishment, on the ground that all alliance between the civil and religious power was indefensible. In point of fact, their real purpose was, to destroy both the Establishment and the State, and to substitute therefor a kingdom of the "saints," in which Church and State should be merged into one. It may be said, however, that with this phase of Puritanism we have but little concern. It soon ran its course under the Commonwealth, — a movement, which, while it signalized the greatness of its leaders, will always be ranked as one of the completest failures in history. Nor need we make more than a passing reference to that noted colony of separatists, which, leaving Northern England, went first to Amsterdam, and then to Leyden, and from thence despatched the illustrious little company of Pilgrims which came in "The Mayflower" to these shores. No one can be insensible to the romantic and poetic interest that belongs to the goodly little band, who, throughout the whole course of their wanderings, set an example of constancy, and greatness of soul, that were worthy of the faith's best ages, — of whom their pious leader well said, that "they knew they were pilgrims, and looked not much on the things of earth, but lifted up their eyes to heaven, their dearest country, and quieted their spirits."[1]

[1] Bancroft: History of the United States, vol. i. p. 235.

Deeply touched, however, as all must be, by the idyllic grace of the story of the Pilgrims, and pleasant as it is to linger over it, yet candor compels us to acknowledge, that the true genesis of New-England colonial life is not to be traced to Plymouth, and that the Pilgrims had no direct and but little indirect influence in shaping its later development. The true beginning of New-England colonial life was originally projected by Arthur Lake, Bishop of Bath and Wells, one of the Puritan prelates of the English Church. So greatly was the bishop interested in the movement, that he declared, shortly before his death, that "he would go himself, but for his age."[1] The plan projected by him was carried out later by his coadjutor and friend, the Rev. John White, "the patriarch minister of Dorchester," and, like Lake, a Puritan, but not a separatist, who, with Roger Conant, succeeded in 1625 in planting the colony of Salem on the Bay of Massachusetts.[2]

[1] Bancroft: History of the United States, vol. i. p. 264. Also A Dying Father's Last Legacy to an Only Child; or, Mr. Hugh Peters's Advice to His Daughter, pp. 101, 102, London, 1660. Also Felt's Ecclesiastical History of New England, pp. 79, 80. It is to be noted, that this important statement is in the *latest*, but not in the earlier, editions of Bancroft.

[2] Bancroft: History of the United States, vol. i. p. 264.

Few, if any, of the original colonists were separatists. Among their leaders and most active supporters were the Rev. Samuel Skelton of Clare Hall, Cambridge; and the Rev. Francis Higginson of Jesus College, Cambridge, both in English orders, though Puritans.[1] It is to be noted, moreover, that, soon after the later settlement of the colony at Boston, none but clergymen in regular orders were elected and set apart to minister to the congregation.[2] Soon afterwards, indeed, the churches of the colony proceeded to elaborate an organization different from that of the English Church, and more in accordance with the organization of the Independents; but it is easy to see that this was designed at first to be a departure, rather from the organization of the Establishment than from the Church's order. Two of their number, John and Samuel Browne, protested against even this departure; and they were promptly silenced and expelled: but, in doing this, the Puritans declared that their purpose was, to separate, "not from the Church of England, but from its

---

[1] Prince: p. 191 (note).
[2] Bancroft: History of the United States, vol. i. pp. 271, 182. Prince: p. 191 (note).

corruptions."[1] At the re-organization of the structure of the colony a little later, when the home council transferred "the government of the colony to those who should inhabit there,"[2] John Winthrop of Groton in Sussex, a Churchman and a conformist, though a Puritan, was elected governor; and he soon drew around him a large number of like-minded men, whose purpose was, not to separate from either Church or State, but to realize the Puritan ideal of an alliance between them.[3] Under the fresh impulse given by Winthrop and his companions, the Colony of Massachusetts Bay began to shape the destiny of New England. Boston was chosen as the seat of government; and the First Church of Boston was organized by electing the Rev. John Wilson for their pastor, who, while submitting to the imposition of their hands as a solemn setting apart for his work, refused to renounce the regular orders already received by him in England.[4] Thus it was that Puritanism was transplanted to these shores, and

[1] Bancroft: History of the United States, vol. i. pp. 272, 273.
[2] Ibid. p. 274.
[3] Bancroft: History of the United States, vol. i. pp. 277, 278. Palfrey: History of New England, vol. i. pp. 311-313.
[4] Bancroft: History of the United States, vol. i. p. 282.

began its career here, not as a separation from the English Church, but as a movement towards the attainment of that control of the State by the "elect" which had come to be the object of Puritan ambition.

As time passed on, this object eclipsed all others. In 1631 the Puritans proceeded to enact, that "no man for the time to come should be admitted to the freedom of the body politic but such as are members of some of the churches within the limits of the same." "Thus," says Bancroft, "the body became a theocracy: God himself was to govern his people; and the 'saints by calling,' whose names an immutable decree had registered from eternity as the objects of divine love, whose election had been visibly manifested by their conscious experience of religion in the heart, whose aim was confirmed by the most solemn compact formed with heaven and one another around the memorials of a crucified Redeemer, were, by the fundamental laws of the colony, constituted the oracle of the divine will."[1] The same writer also calls it "the reign of the visible Church, a commonwealth of the

[1] Bancroft: History of the United States, vol. i. p. 288.

chosen people in covenant with God." [1] To the more complete and speedy realization of this theocratic purpose, the Puritans proceeded to sacrifice the religious ties that bound them to the mother Church. Whoever opposed or refused to fall in with their plans, was set upon, punished, and expelled. Roger Williams, one of the purest and most gifted souls of that or any age, was ignominiously exiled because he pleaded for liberty of conscience. Quakers were proscribed and banished. Tender and gentle Quaker women were scourged.[2] Nonconformity was treated as treason; and a tyranny more inexorable and severe than that with which the Establishment, in its most persecuting days, had visited dissent, was set up by the Puritans in New England. Whoever will study the annals of the New-England colonies, and the long lists, both of Churchmen and nonconformists, who suffered for conscience in early colonial days, will see that Puritanism, with all its stern virtues, was not the friend, but the foe, of liberty; and that its sons and daughters passed on to freedom, not because, but in spite, of their creed.

[1] Bancroft: History of the United States, vol. i. p. 288.
[2] George Bishop: New England Judged, p. 50. London, 1703.

As the instinct of civil liberty was strong enough among the Puritans themselves to overcome the narrow bigotry of their religious and political opinions, so the cause of religious liberty was gradually relieved of its worst hinderances. Among the causes which contributed to this result, a prominent place must be assigned to the influence of Roger Williams and the generous spirits associated with him, who, from the secure protection afforded by the little commonwealth of Rhode Island and Providence Plantation, organized and directed a ceaseless propagandism against the stern policy of their neighbors. But the most important was the gradual decay of Puritanism itself, the exhaustion of its energy, the spending of its force. Like all mere schools of opinion, it could not last. Like all mere human systems, it waxed old, and was ready to vanish away. From the time when it finally separated from the Church's order, it began to lose its consistency, and to evaporate its early spirit; and it eventually came to pass, that large numbers of its people re-acted into open or covert Unitarianism, or other forms of liberalism and indifference. At the time of the American Revolution, Puritanism, as such, did not have a word to say for itself in the councils of the Continental Congress. The shackles of bigotry had already fallen from the people's minds. Though the forms of theocratic tyranny remained long unrepealed, and though the spirit of it still manifests itself in many kinds of restless propagandism; yet the mass of the New-England people grew up unconsciously into a better freedom, both civil and religious, than their leaders aimed at, and, like their brethren in every colony, builded wiser than they knew.

The influence of Quakerism on the growth and development of our religious liberty is a subject of surpassing interest, deserving of far more time and space than can be here accorded to it. It must suffice to point out, that its noblest function was amply discharged in its earliest days. Then it was the apostleship of universal toleration; and it retaught the great lessons of the gospel, so long obscured or forgotten, of the mightiness of meekness, the dignity of conscience, the royalty of self-sacrifice. Nothing had been seen in this world for more than a thousand years so beautiful as the spirit of early Quakerism, as manifested in George Fox and William Penn. There was profound truth, as well as touching sweetness, in the eulogy which the latter pronounced when he heard of the former's death: "Many Friends have done virtuously, but thou, George, hast excelled them all!" There is no brighter page in political history than that which tells of the generous enterprise of William Penn in founding and long sustaining this great commonwealth and this noble metropolis. Long may it be before his memory shall cease to be venerated here, and his quiet spirit to pervade the social and public life of this City of Brotherly Love! Yet, when we come to study Quakerism as a movement, we find that it contained in its bosom a germ of subtle hostility to the very religious liberty which it honestly professed to serve. It contemned the Church's order, and renounced her sacraments. It refused to acknowledge any external religious authority. It insisted that all that was reasonable in objective Christianity was capable of being embodied in the institutions of civil society, and it insisted on respecting nothing that was not so embodied. So it came to pass, that its toleration was seen to mean little more than a philosophical forbearance; and that its spirit would have led, if uncontrolled, to a contemptuous sweeping away of all religious systems whatever, — to a complete secularization of Christianity. Such a tendency was well designed to abolish the Church, but manifestly it could not have been trusted to establish relations between it and civil society.

Lastly, we must consider briefly the effect of Anglicanism, meaning by this term the attachment of colonial Churchmen to the English Establishment. Undoubtedly, the first attitude of Anglicanism in Virginia and the Carolinas, and later in Maryland and New York, was hostile to religious liberty. No word of excuse shall ever be offered by me for the proscription for opinion's sake which was enacted in those colonies. And yet it cannot be denied, that such proscription was rather political than religious, and always lacked the bitterness of religious fanaticism. The consequence was, that, as fast as the Anglican colonists outgrew their original subserviency to political prerogative, their proscriptive enactments fell into complete desuetude. Hence it was that Anglicanism did not retard the development of religious liberty to the same extent, and in the same way, as was done by the stern Puritanism of Massachusetts Bay. Allusion has already been made to the fact, that it was in Virginia that the Declaration of Rights, which was the first authoritative proclamation of civil and religious liberty in any land, was enacted; that it was written by George Mason, a devout communicant of the Church; and that it was unanimously adopted by the Virginia House of Burgesses, the large majority of whom were also Churchmen. That Churchmen should thus take the lead was no accident. It was easier for a Churchman to sever the alliance between religion and civil society, because to him Christianity stood on ground altogether different from that occupied by the State. He believed that the Church was a theocracy, instituted and upheld by a living King; and that Christianity, being the Church's concern, did not need to either lean upon or to control the State. Having come to understand that the State is purely secular, while the Church is altogether spiritual; that the State is altogether human, and the Church altogether divine,—he had no fears that either the one or the other would suffer by the separation. Therefore it was perfectly natural that George Mason, the

Churchman, should have written the Declaration which was the true charter of our national freedom; and there was a natural fitness in the fact, that the Continental Congress, which began the work of achieving our freedom, was opened with prayer by a clergyman of the Church, and that the patriot army which won our freedom was commanded by a son of the Church. In strict consistency with the same line of events, the Church, being rescued here for the first time in long centuries from the burden and the tyranny of State control, began a gracious career in this country after the war, and gave singular evidence, by the promptness and completeness with which she adapted her organization to the framework of the State, by the readiness with which she took up her great work, by her cordial sympathy with our free institutions, and by a consistent policy of non-interference with all questions merely civic and political, that this free land is the Church's home; that she has found here the liberty for which her children long had sighed in every clime; and that she is able, by reason of her divinely constituted polity and her unchanging order, to serve the commonwealth without being enslaved by it, and to help it without intruding into its councils, or interfering with its power. Hither, then, to the asylum of liberty, the refuge of the oppressed, came the Church of God. Long Pope-ridden in former centuries, long State-ridden in the mother-land, here the chains fell from her limbs; and it will be her gracious part in the future, as in the past, to testify to her sense of the sacredness of her own freedom, and of the freedom of the State, by exemplifying in her history the answer of her King, who said of old, "My kingdom is not of this world." "My kingdom is not from hence."

Historically, then, we have seen that the relation of Christianity to civil society in this land is not the relation which Puritanism would have chosen; nor is it that which Quakerism would have preferred; nor yet is it that which is exemplified in the English Establishment. The actual outcome has been perfect religious liberty. And this arises, not from the toleration of all religions alike by a State, which, in tolerating, assumes to patronize them all; nor does it arise out of a mere equilibrium of religious or sectarian forces, the prudent refusal of the State to interfere among warring factions; but it arises out of the very conception of civil society as a social compact between men acting in obedience to the moral and social instincts of their nature, and deriving all civil authority from the consent of the governed. In a word, it is because the State is here placed upon a purely secular basis that all alliance with, or patronage of, or control over or control by, Christianity as a spiritual religion is impossible. In order to change this, it would be necessary to remodel the State, — to make it something different from what it now is; and to do this would be to utterly overthrow our liberty. I believe that the relation of Christianity to civil society in this country is the ideal relation that was present to the thought of Jesus. I believe that all Christian history has been leading up to the possibility of the establishment of this relation. I believe that it is being more and more realized as Christians awake to the fact that the State is secular and human, and that the Church is spiritual and divine. But I believe that there are tendencies abroad, some re-actionary and others radical in their character, which gravely threaten to suspend it, if not to destroy it altogether. Let us recur for a moment to a definition of that relation which has been suggested already, and then indicate some of the dangers which threaten it.

Christianity, then, is personal loyalty to Christ as a divine and living king, manifested in the obedience of discipleship, and maintained by communion with him in sacrament and prayer. Into this relation with Christ, man is called as an individual: he enters into it by faith and through grace. By it he is recognized as the only ethical subject. By its cult he is individualized, dignified, saved. Yet the inevitable effect of this is, to bind him more closely to his kind; to develop his social instinct into love for his neighbor; and to enable him to find his own completeness, not in isolation from his fellows, but in association with them, — not in selfishness, but in brotherly kindness. Christianity, then, begins with Christ, and, through the individual, leads back to him. Civil society, on the other hand, begins with the individual. It has its genesis in the social instincts and needs of the individual man, who, combining with others in obedience to those instincts, and in order to serve those needs, proceeds to organize an instrumentality which shall serve the common purposes which he and his associates have in view; which instrumentality he calls a State, or government, or civil society. But this civil society, having its genesis in man, and deriving its authority from him, has its excellence measured solely by its capacity to serve him, and finds its end in him. At this point, then, and at this point alone, namely, in the individual, Christianity and civil society touch each other. The great concern of Christianity is the culture of the individual man, the training of him for immortality. But inasmuch as man can, by reason of the social characteristics of his nature, attain to his true individuality only in association with his fellows, and inasmuch as it is the effect of Christianity to enlarge man's social instincts, and expand as well as dignify man's social nature, Christianity enters through this culture into the most intimate relations with civil society. Nevertheless, in pursuing this culture, Christianity is not only protected by its origin and authority from all control by the State, but it is prohibited, by the very character of its legitimate influence, from exercising any control over the State. For to control the State would be to destroy man's political nature, and to defeat the impulses towards society which its design, as we have seen, is to re-enforce, and not to abrogate or destroy. From this it appears that a theocratic Church and a secular State mutually so limit each other as to forbid the interference of each with the other.

There are, however, three tendencies abroad which aim at the disturbance of this adjustment, and which, in the event of the complete success of any one of them, must destroy it altogether. Our limits will allow us only to refer to them in the briefest way. The first of these may be described as the surviving political spirit of Puritanism. We have seen how the Puritans at first aimed at nothing short of the control of the State by the Church, the subordination of the civil to the ecclesiastical power. We have also seen how the organized movement to effect this purpose was gradually relaxed, and its avowed objects more and more discredited, until, after a long struggle, the so-called ecclesiastical statutes of some of the New-England States were repealed within the present century. Nevertheless, the spirit of it survives, and still carries on a restless propagandism; the object being, on the part of various religious bodies, to secure control of the State as such, and to use political instrumentalities on the one hand to secure religious ends, while religious instrumentalities, on the other, are pledged and employed to gain or to serve political ends. I need not specify instances in which this has been attempted, and is still attempted. I need not name religious bodies, which, by their corporate action, have undertaken to influence legislation or to win elections. It is notorious that such things have been done; so that there have been eras in our history when it seemed that the practical politics of the land have been dictated by ecclesiastical conferences, and when politicians were obnoxious to the charge of shaping their utterances and their actions to meet the views and secure the support of large and influential religious denominations which had undertaken such dictatorship. Of such interference on the part of religious bodies, it is not too much to say, that it tends to the utter subversion of both civil and religious liberty. Not only is it a violation of the only relation which Christ intended should subsist, as we have seen, between Christianity and civil society, but its inevitable effect must be to eventually abrogate the true authority of both. By thrusting religion into politics, the true idea of the Church is impaired. By substituting religious or ecclesiastical for civil reasons of State, the true doctrine of popular sovereignty in political government is overthrown, and the principle of despotism in politics is practically inaugurated. The final result must be, the degradation of religion and the depravation of politics, the destruction of the true character of the Church on the one hand, and of the State on the other. Against this danger it behooves the Christian citizen of the Republic to watch with jealous care. Already it has worked much evil, and it portends even greater evil in the future. The proper spheres of Church and State are distinct. The only safety for either lies in the maintenance of their entire independence and separateness each from the other. The moment either invades the province of the other, it becomes a wrongdoer, no matter what the alleged motive may be. In a word, the true function of Christian statesmanship is the maintenance of the relation instituted by Christ between Christianity and civil society.

The second movement hostile to civil and religious liberty may be even more briefly referred to, for the reason that it is organized, tangible, historic, and is therefore better known. It may be designated as Ultramontanism or Vaticanism in politics and religion. It is in no spirit of the mere alarmist that I point out the enormous dangers which threaten us from this source. No examination of the relation between Christianity and civil society can escape the portentous fact, that, in this land, a vast multitude of our fellow-citizens are committed by their creed to a denial of the fundamental principles upon which our government is founded, and are pledged by the irreformable teachings, and, indeed, mandates, of their religion, to regard as the ideal State, a State that has been made practically subject to a foreign and irresponsible ecclesiastical power. It is but fair to admit that this was not always so. Though the Roman Catholics of the colonies cannot be said to have played any part, as such, in the achievement and settlement of our civil and religious liberty; yet their loyalty to the cause of the country could not be doubted: and there were no more devoted patriots than some of the wise, good, and great men among their number. It has been well pointed out, that the establishment of religious toleration in Maryland, while "it was a wise measure, for which the two Lords Baltimore, father and son, deserve the highest honor," yet "the measure was really defensive; and its main and very legitimate purpose plainly was, to secure the free exercise of the Roman-Catholic religion."[1] It is also evident, that the enactment of toleration was not the work of Roman Catholics in Maryland; since toleration was provided for in the charter which the English king granted them, and the colonial Act of Toleration was passed by a legislative body, of which two-thirds were Protestants.[2] It is, however, undoubtedly true, we think, that the spirit which for a long time animated the Roman Catholics of this country was not antagonistic to our institutions. Though, beyond all question, the attitude of the Papacy, especially since the publication by Boniface VIII. of his famous bull, *Unam Sanctam*, had been hostile to popular liberty and the independence of the civil power; yet in this country the circum-

[1] Gladstone: Vaticanism.
[2] Gladstone: Rome and the Newest Fashions in Religion. Preface, pp. viii, ix. Also Maryland Not a Roman Catholic Colony, by E. D. N., p. 7.

stances favorable to freedom had been sufficiently influential to keep our Roman-Catholic population virtually true to their civic allegiance. But since the Vatican Council, and the promulgation of the Vatican decrees, all this is changed. Since the decree of infallibility, a theory of civil society absolutely inconsistent with the principles upon which our institutions are founded has been imposed by irreformable authority upon all who belong to the Roman obedience; and an authoritative declaration of ecclesiastical and civil rights and duties, and of the relation between them, has been made, which is in conflict with the principles and policy of our government. To the reply, that there is a sense in which the Canon Law may be interpreted which is not inconsistent with the duties of American citizenship, it is enough to answer, that, even if this were so, the power to interpret all canons, and to define all human duty, is now declared, as an article of faith, to be lodged in an infallible, irresponsible, and foreign potentate, who may, if he so please, promulgate to-morrow, as his predecessors have done again and again in time past, such definitions as will set all who accept them at open variance with civil society. To this it is no answer to say that he will not do so; that he will be restrained by any considerations of truth, of justice, or by any influence of a spiritual and supernatural character. The very recognition of his right, of his power, to do this, at once destroys undivided allegiance to the State, and transfers the true and ultimate authority upon which society rests to the Roman *curia*. This is the only tenable theory of Vaticanism; and, however vociferously it may be disavowed, it is the theory upon which the Roman-Catholic hierarchy in this country are obviously acting.[1] Bishops receiving mission and jurisdiction immediately from Rome, and responsible directly to Rome and to Rome only, assisted by a clergy completely subject to them and to the Pope, many of whom are aliens by birth and education, and all of whom are separated by the discipline of order and the celibacy of their lives from the domestic life of the people, — these constitute the agencies by which Rome is able to carry on any kind of propagandism in this country. When we add to this consideration the further

---

[1] For one of the latest evidences of this, see the Pastoral Letter, published at the Fourth Provincial Council of Cincinnati, March 19, 1882.

fact, that the spiritual control which Romanism as a system exerts over the consciences, the words, the thoughts, the actions, of its adherents is indefeasible and complete, and that it is through this control that the Roman pontiff now claims the power to enforce his definitions of all kinds of human duty, it is seen what a tremendous engine of power is here provided, and how portentous of evil it would be to our free country unless its influence should be neutralized. That it will be neutralized I do not doubt. But it must be by the most zealous care to diffuse intelligence; to build up true religion, especially in the homes of the land; and to promote the promulgation of right views of the relation between Christianity and civil society.

Finally, there is a re-actionary movement, provoked in great degree by the tendencies already noted, which, for want of a better term, may be called secularism. Unlike English secularism, it is not disposed to enter the arena of theological debate; though some of its advocates are not unwilling to masquerade on the lecture-platform as theologasters for gain. It is for the most part a quiet, unavowed purpose on the part of politicians, both active and theoretical, who are either irreligious, or indifferent to all religion, to discredit the Christian Church, to limit, by unfriendly legislation, its activities and agencies, and finally dismiss it with contempt, or reduce it to entire subjection to the civil power. The theory on which it proceeds is, that the Church is to be tolerated only because it serves, or if it serves social and political order. It is not denied, that it may be useful to amuse the ignorant and restrain the vicious; but it is insisted, that, in doing this, it only wins a right to be tolerated by the State as useful to it, unless, indeed, it can be made a mere department of the State, to "evolve its ethics;" in which case it is gravely proposed to take it into the pay of the State, to subsidize it, and control it altogether. It is pointed out, that religion under our present voluntary system is altogether too expensive. The State could maintain a clergy of its own at half the cost. It is estimated, that, in this country, religion costs the people one dollar and ten cents *per capita* per annum; whereas in France, where the clergy are supported by the State, clerical salaries are very much smaller, and the tax on the people very much less. This and other reasons combine to strengthen the movement to which reference is made.[1] No doubt, there is as yet a lack of unity and organization among its adherents: but they are all animated by a growing hostility to the Church, and to the clergy as a class; and they do not lack opportunities to make their power felt. The character of 'the danger from this source cannot be overstated. It is the most remorseless, the most unsparing, the most cruel, political movement that has been instituted in modern times. If it should succeed, it could not crush out Christianity, of course; but it would convert the State into a despotism the most intolerable. The extent of the danger is easily underestimated. Unless I greatly mistake the signs of the times, it will soon appear to be one of the gravest perils of our national political life. Nevertheless, the remedy is easily discernible. The evils against which it is re-actionary must be avoided.[2] The pretensions of Puritanism and Vaticanism in

---

[1] See A Critical Review of American Politics, by Charles Reemelin, p. 326 *et seq.*

[2] The reader is referred, for an illustration of the dangers and evils here pointed out, to a recent debate in the French Chambers between the Bishop of Angers and M. Roche, reported in The Guardian newspaper of Nov. 15, 1882.

politics must be discredited and overthrown. The political preacher and the political priest should be relegated by public opinion to their proper duties. The same public opinion should be taught to utterly discredit and frown down all interference with religious liberty and the rights of conscience on the hustings and in the legislature. If it be asked, Who shall undertake to do this for religion and the State? may I not answer, Churchmen will undertake to do their part towards it? Churchmen occupy the vantage-ground, and a large responsibility rests upon them in this as in all things. For, if we have reached right conclusions in the matter, whatever limitations other religious bodies labor under, American Churchmen are free to hold true views of the relations between Christianity and civil society.

LECTURE IV.

EDUCATION.

LECTURE IV.

EDUCATION.

> "And Jesus came and spake unto them, saying, All power is given unto me in heaven and in earth. Go ye therefore, and teach all nations, baptizing them in the name of the Father, and of the Son, and of the Holy Ghost: teaching them to observe all things whatsoever I have commanded you: and, lo, I am with you alway, even unto the end of the world." — ST. MATTHEW xxviii. 18-20.

WHEN we consider how completely our Lord committed his work to his apostles, leaving them to carry out in history and time his magnificent and far-reaching purposes, we reasonably expect to find, among his parting injunctions to them, some indication of the relation which his Church was intended to sustain to the various conditions by which it was to be surrounded. We are prepared, therefore, to see, in what has been well called the great commission, the outline, at least, of a general plan that was to guide the Church's activity in all ages and lands. It is evident, indeed, upon a little reflection, that very much more than a bare outline is here suggested.

It is quite certain, that, however brief and practical the apostolical commission was as a missionary mandate and working-charter, it was pregnant with a wealth of meaning that could be fully disclosed to human thought, only in the developments of history. We may well believe that the "infinite abundance" of that meaning has not yet been fully revealed; but enough has been already made known to exemplify how clearly and completely all the questions which have emerged along the line of the Church's work were present in the beginning to the thought of the Church's Founder. It was as the King and Sovereign Ruler of all things that he spoke, investing his agents and apostles with complete and plenary authority; but it was also as the great statesman of humankind, as one who took note of the conditions that were before him, and who knew how to adjust his agencies to the work which they were to perform, and to the circumstances by which they were to be surrounded. Regarding the apostolic commission, then, as the charter of the Church's work, we find a suggestion of the various employments of which that work was to be composed; and among these it is here indicated that the

Church was intended to discharge an educational or pedagogic function towards the nations, and to enter into a relation the most intimate and influential with civil society.

There is a characteristic connection between our Lord's assumption of universal power, and the missionary and pedagogic mandate which he based upon it. He still maintained his renunciation of a kingdom of force. He persisted in his high resolve, that his kingdom should not be of this world, even while he proclaimed that all power, both in heaven and earth, had been given to him. In the fulness of that power he sent his apostles forth, not to reign, nor to fight; not to oppose force to force; not to subjugate or destroy; but to disciple, to teach, to win men, and transform them by nurture and grace. It seemed a strange *non sequitur* to the philosophic and civic thought of that age, and men have hardly yet learned clearly to discern the force of the divine logic upon which the "therefore" of the great commission is founded. It was because all power, both in heaven and in earth, had been given to him: it was because he spoke, not merely as man, but as God, that he persisted in the day of his exaltation, as in the time of his humiliation, in the divine method of winning men, discarding and discrediting authority and force as of no real value in the kingdom of souls. Certainly, never man spake like this man. For man, in the day of his power, has thought it royal to exercise dominion and enforce authority: but Jesus said, All power is mine; therefore go ye and disciple the nations, baptizing them; go teach them: and this my work and purpose I will also participate in as I lead and direct you; for I will be with you alway, even unto the end of the world.

The terms of the apostolic commission indicate that the Christian Church has a mission to the nations of the earth. At the same time, it is clearly implied that the Church was not intended to operate directly upon the nations as such, nor to enter into alliance with them, or lord it over them. For, when we come to inquire how the apostles were to disciple the nations, we find that it was to be done through the nurture, the discipline, the teaching, which, in the nature of the case, could be applied only to the individuals of which nations are composed. Christian discipleship cannot be other than personal. It is only as a free and self-determining personality that a man can become a disciple of the Lord Jesus. We have seen, that it was one of the distinguishing characteristics of the plan of Christ that he recognized and appealed to the individuality of man. This characteristic was not obscured in the terms of the apostolic commission. One by one the souls were to be baptized. One by one they were to be taught to observe the things which he commanded, and in this way the nation was to be discipled. For man, as we have seen, is a social, or, as Aristotle terms him, a "political," being. He is endowed with a strong impulse to associate with his fellows for the attainment of certain definite political objects. The association which actually results from the operation of this common impulse constitutes the nation, the State. The way, then, to reach the nation, according to the terms of the apostolical commission, is through the constituent elements out of which it is organized, and along the lines of its organization. Disciple the men, the souls, baptizing them. Teach them to observe the things which Christ commanded. In this way the nations shall be discipled, and made the kingdoms of God and of his

Christ. It is most interesting to note, that the very terms of the apostolic commission are inconsistent with any other theory of civil society than that which is here adopted. If the State were organized from above, and not from beneath, then the Church's operations would have been directed primarily to the nation at such, or at least to the rulers thereof. It would have been sufficient to disciple the king, or the head of the people, first, leaving the rest to follow as the result of governmental influence and authority. In point of fact, this method has been attempted, in more than one instance of missionary enterprise, as the natural result of a false theory of civil society. More than one despotic ruler has committed the blunder of attempting to impose Christianity upon his people by royal mandate, or by the influence of the royal example; but, in every such instance, a speedy apostasy has demonstrated the falsity of the method and of the civic theory upon which it was founded. The apostolic commission, however, points out a more excellent way. Disciple the nations, it says in effect, by the Christian nurture and Christian teaching of individual souls. Direct your efforts to the source of civic authority and power. Translate the souls of men into the kingdom of God. Make the men who compose society to be more and more what Christ would have them to be. Stand beside the fountains of national life, and keep them pure. In this way fashion the characters of men, create public opinion, transform and transfigure the ideals by which men are chiefly led. Nay, transform and transfigure men themselves, so that their social and political instincts and impulses may take the right direction, and pursue the right course. In this way the nations shall be discipled, and brought to acknowledge him to whom all power has been given in heaven and in earth.

It is evident, then, that the influence exerted by Christianity upon civil society would be intimate and profound in precise proportion to the completeness with which the Christian Church performs the duty which is here indicated. And in a country like ours, whose government derives its authority, not only in abstract theory, but in actual fact, from the popular will, the obvious method of attempting to shape the character of society, and to disciple the nation, is to apply Christian influence to the very source of the nation's power and authority; that is, to the wills and consciences of the people themselves. It becomes, therefore, a matter of the greatest practical importance, to inquire how Christian influence may best be exerted in the nurture, the training, the education, of a people. In a word, we are brought, in the course of our inquiry, to one of the most important practical questions of the day, which is, What is the relation of Christianity to civil society in the matter of education?

If we use the word education in its broadest sense, it indicates the most comprehensive and the most precious of all human interests. Every human being has an indefeasible right to be educated; that is, to have his faculties developed, to be put in possession of his powers, and to have the use of himself at his best. And, in order that this right might be realized by each soul, God himself has instituted a sacred economy, which he founded upon the most profound and cogent instincts of humanity, — which is the economy of the family. For this he instituted marriage in the very beginning of human history. Nay, in the very act of creation, and in delivering to man his viceregal sovereignty over the world, God instituted marriage, and sanctified it as the means by which man was at once to realize and perpetuate his dominion. For this cause he created man male and female, and "blessed them, and said unto them, Be fruitful, and multiply, and replenish the earth, and subdue it." For this cause he ordained the inviolability and indissolubility of marriage; decreeing that a man shall "leave his father and his mother, and shall cleave unto his wife: and they shall be one flesh." Undoubtedly, marriage is a divine mystery, whose ultimate basis lies among the secret things that belong to the Lord our God. But it is also a vocation. "When God created mankind male and female, he thereby announced, and, as it were, impressed upon our nature, the fact that it was his will that we should marry. Hence we are justified in saying that marriage is a duty, and the most universal duty incumbent on us."[1] And, among the obligations which impose the duty of marriage on mankind, none is more cogent than this, that in this way God has intended to provide, not only for the perpetuity, but for the education, of the race. The most lofty and dignified use of the family is the

---

[1] Luthardt: Moral Truths of Christianity, p. 114.

fit nurture and education of the children given to wedded love, and the great and sacred responsibility of educating such children rests primarily and by divine enactment upon the parents. It is the design of our heavenly Father, that every child born into the world should spend its nascent years in the calm peace of a holy home, protected, nourished, and prepared for the duties and responsibilities of life, by parental care. When this is borne in mind, we realize how precious the sanctity of the home-life is, and how inviolable those safeguards ought to be by which Providence has surrounded it. We realize why it is that God has decreed that marriage, once consummated, should be indissoluble except by death. For marriage was designed, in the divine economy, not merely, nor even chiefly, for the ease or comfort of the wedded pair, but for the maintenance and education of their children. The home is the sanctuary appointed by God, within whose sacredness immortal souls appear as visitants from the skies, and within whose order and peace such souls are to be nurtured and trained for a useful passage through time, and a worthy return to immortality. He, therefore, who invades its sanctity, or disturbs its peace, is not only a transgressor of the divine law, but is also guilty of the greatest conceivable crime against society at its very source. How monstrous, then, are the laws which legalize confusion and disorder in the family, by loosening the bonds of matrimony, and permitting the wayward passions of men to break up an economy which God intended should be indissoluble!

The family, then, is the divinely appointed institution for the education of the human race; and the duty of educating every child rests primarily upon its parents. This obligation preceded the establishment of civil society, and was in full force long before Christianity began its work among men. It is important for us to remember, that education has been intrusted by divine appointment, neither to the Church nor to the State, but to the family, — to an institution with which the State cannot rightly interfere, and which the Church must sanctify and protect. Hence the right of every child to an adequate education is not distinctively either a political or a Christian right, however intimately both Christianity and civil society may be related to it : and, conversely, the duty of affording an education to every child is not distinctively a political or a Christian duty; since the duty was imposed, and the means for it provided, antecedent to the formation of society and the institution of Christianity. It is important for us to remember, then, at the outset, that neither the State nor the Church has an original function in the work of education proper, but that, in so far as they have relation to it, they must both enter into such relation through the family.

The relations sustained by the State and by the Church to education, however, are essentially different, as we shall see, — so different that it is quite impossible to co-ordinate them. Whatsoever responsibility and whatsoever authority the State has in the matter of education are wholly delegated, and are limited by the terms of the compact or arrangement by which such delegation is effected. Christianity, on the other hand, approaches education, as it does all human interests, from above, and with a mission, not to usurp its function, or set it aside, but to inform, to spiritualize, to complete it. Christianity is related to education as an influence from another world directed to the whole domain of human well-being; while the State is related to education, only in so far as education may be intrusted to its supervision and control. And it should not be forgotten, that such supervision and control can be made to extend to only a small part of education. For more is learned by the child at home than at school: the most important part, not only of the knowledge acquired by him, but of the development of his faculties, the appropriation of his powers, takes place under the manifold influences of parental authority, parental example, parental affection, and in the atmosphere of the home.[1] Nevertheless, there is a department of mental culture and discipline, the supervision and direction of which can be wisely delegated to others. In other words, teachers may be wisely employed, whose attainments and special training enable them to secure the best results in such culture and discipline; the teachers so employed being merely the agents of the parents, and deriving their authority from them. In order to secure the most efficient teachers, it is in the natural course of things for several families to combine;

[1] Compare Luthardt, Moral Truths of Christianity, p. 144 *et seq.*

in which case it is quite evident that the teacher, as the agent of all such families, would have authority only in those matters which all united in intrusting to him. The case is not at all altered, when, by civil compact or enactment, the citizens of a commonwealth delegate to the State the duty of sustaining and directing some part of their educational work. In this case the State is simply the agent of the families composing it, and has no direct authority and no immediate responsibility beyond what is thus delegated. It is true, that in a representative commonwealth like one of ours, in which popular suffrage is the appointed means of delegating public authority, it is not the family as such, but the citizen at the polls, who creates and controls the agencies of public education. Nevertheless, the citizen, in this case especially, and in every case in some sort, is the representative of the family and home; each citizen being in the natural order the head of a family. The duty, the responsibility, the authority, of the State, then, in public education, are not original, but derived, and are limited strictly to those things which by agreement have been delegated to public control.

In saying this, it is not denied that education is a matter of public concern. On the contrary, it is insisted that it is a matter of paramount public concern that the people of a free State should all be educated. Nevertheless, it is also insisted that the obligation to this rests primarily, not on the State as such, but on those who make and control the State; namely, on the citizens in their domestic relations, who compose the body politic. Because man is a social and political being, he is under obligation, not only to organize civil society, but to make it as efficient as possible; and, in order to this, he is under obligation to promote the virtue and intelligence of those upon whose intelligence and virtue the well-being of the State must depend. There are, therefore, manifold considerations which require the citizen, and the State through him, to promote the diffusion of knowledge, the increase of virtue, the development of intelligence, among the people. In doing this, however, the citizen must be content to employ the State, only in such a way as may be consistent with the economy of civil society. In educational as in other matters, the State ought not to exceed or to abuse its delegated powers. We have seen that all its "just powers are derived from the consent of the governed," and that it has no divine right or inherent authority to transgress or transcend this limitation. Much less may it do so in this matter, which was primarily committed to another institution; namely, the family.

The question as to whether our public schools have any duty or authority in regard to religious culture or instruction, is, first of all, a question of fact. And, as a matter of fact, it is not to be denied, I suppose, that no such duty or authority could be delegated to the State in the present divided condition of religious opinion among our people. To the further question, whether such duty and authority ought to be so delegated, it seems to me that a negative answer must be returned. To teach religion, or to promote religious culture, does not fall within the province of civil society. To discharge these functions the Church of Christ was instituted, and the Church can neither lay down its work nor delegate its responsibility. It was to the Church, and not to the State, that Christ said, Go teach men to observe the things which I have commanded; and, as Churchmen, we are not at liberty, as it seems to me, to intrust the State, or the public schools under the State, with any authority in the matter of religious instruction. Not only would the delegation of such authority be impracticable, but it would be altogether unwise and undesirable. Christian statesmanship, especially in this land, should not be slow to see that such a procedure would be based on a principle altogether at variance with the philosophy of civil society, and which, if accepted, and carried out to its logical conclusion, would speedily overthrow public liberty. For, if the State can be invested with authority to teach religion in the schools, it must be empowered to determine what religion it will teach. If it can be invested with the authority to shape religious convictions, it may also have the power to impose all opinions. To say nothing of the transfer of the Church's function to the State, and the virtual abrogation of the Church, in either case there would be a complete obliteration of the rights of conscience, a complete destruction of personal liberty, and the erection of a tyranny as complete as has yet been accomplished in history.

It is important to remember, that the committal of educational interests to State control is simply a conventional expedient. It is done because it seems best to the body politic, on the whole, that it should be done. The advantages of it are undeniable, but there are also serious disadvantages. Among the disadvantages is the unavoidable exclusion of Christian worship and corresponding direct religious influences from the public school. Certainly, no Christian man can be entirely content with any system of education in which Christian worship is not possible. Beyond all doubt, the ideal school is the school which shall be entirely open on all sides to a genuine Christian influence, to which Christianity is related as a pervading spirit, affecting the children through worship, through discipline, through the example, the character, the unconscious grace, of the teacher. The ideal common school, in other words, is the Christian school, — the school that is Christian, not by virtue of its dogmatic teaching, nor by virtue of any special ecclesiastical control, but by virtue of its being pervaded, through worship and discipline, in tone and character, by a genuine Christian spirit. Now, it is undeniable that these advantages cannot be secured by civil enactment; and they cannot be secured by State control. And it is certainly most gratifying in every way, that there should be so strong a movement on foot, especially among Churchmen, to establish and maintain, wherever it is practicable, parochial and other religious schools. With such schools, however, our present inquiry has nothing to do. We are now concerned to inquire how Christianity is related to civil society in regard to the common and necessarily secular schools of the country.

The question remains, then, Is it safe, is it right, to intrust the education of our children under any circumstances to schools which must of necessity refrain from religious teaching? To this I believe an affirmative answer may be returned, provided the legitimate influence of Christianity be otherwise brought to bear upon education. To the question whether this is possible under a system of public education that is purely secular, I answer, that I believe it to be entirely possible, provided the Christian Church will recognize its real responsibility, and do its whole duty. It is not a question whether Christian influence shall be withdrawn or banished from the nurture of the young. The question is, whether the young can be adequately nurtured and instructed in religion unless the school in which they spend a few hours each day be enlisted in that particular service. Surely it is not necessary that the family and the Church should delegate their religious duty, or abdicate their spiritual responsibility, to the school; and, in case this is not done, it surely is possible that Christianity may still reach and influence the education of the child through the agencies of Christian nurture and the ordinances of religion in the Church and in the home.

I am aware that the question here proposed is a large, and in many respects a difficult, one. I cannot hope to consider all the issues, both of fact and of opinion, that have arisen along the course of this vexed controversy. All I can hope to do is, to indicate the principles that may lead, as I trust, to its solution. Perhaps we shall gain a more definite idea of the real issues involved if we recur for a moment to a proposition that has been already advanced. We have seen that the obligation to educate the young is older than Christianity; that Christianity did not create this obligation, but found it in full force, — a divinely appointed institution, namely, the family, having been established to discharge it. To educate the human race in this sense was not one of the characteristic duties of the Christian Church; though beyond all question it was to be the Church's mission to re-enforce, encourage, and exalt the agencies that had already been provided for that purpose. It is to be noted, moreover, that of the two different terms that are translated "teach," "teaching," in our version, the first means more properly to "disciple," to bring to discipleship, to make disciples of; and this, as we have seen, has reference to the nation through the Christian nurture of the individuals of which it is composed. The second term, which means teach or instruct in what might be termed the didactic sense of the word, is limited in its application to those things which Christ had taught to the apostles, — "teaching them to observe all things whatsoever I have commanded you." Bearing this fact in mind, then, we are quite prepared to find that there are departments of education which lie quite outside of the special province of Christianity, and that it may be possible for Christianity to be related to such departments without usurpation and without antagonism. In saying this, I do not mean to deny that Christianity must take a deep concern in this as in all human interests; but I wish to point out, that there is a large part of what we call education, especially in the common schools of the land, that the Christian Church is under no necessary obligation to demand the control of. I suppose it is actually the case, that most teachers, even the most devout, in our common schools, have little real occasion to introduce Christian instruction into the classroom. If the facts were known, it would probably be found, that, in the proper work of the school, there is hardly any Christian instruction possible, and that what is given could be better and more effectively given, by the pastor and the parents, in the Church and in the home. It should not be forgotten, that Christianity is not a philosophy. It has no peculiar system of thought, or summary of knowledge. It does not really profess to teach a peculiar astronomy or geology, or cosmogony or ontology, however mistakenly or persistently such a claim has been made for it. Nay, it is now well seen, that however valuable dogmas and creeds are and shall be, yet Christianity is not merely a set of dogmas, or creed of opinions, but is a faith, a life.

It does its best work, not by dogmatic teaching, not by propounding theories of astronomy or geology or cosmogony or ontology, but by touching the heart, arousing the conscience, awakening the spirit to the unseen realities above it and the immortal dignities before it; by giving to the disciple love to be the moral motive-power of his life, and by training him to walk with his unseen Guide and King. And this it does, not necessarily by invading the schoolroom, and inaugurating a special propagandism there, but rather by shedding its radiance over the life of the child, by sanctifying his sabbaths, by the sweet and gentle ministries of the domestic fireside and the family circle, by the simple and loving methods of Christian nurture in the Church, the Sunday school, the home. To be a Christian does not depend upon the amount or the kind of philosophic or scientific knowledge we acquire, nor upon the intellectual training and discipline which we undergo; but it depends on the power of our faith, the completeness of our trust, the entireness of our self-surrender to the guidance of Christ and his Holy Spirit. Let the home-training of the child, then, be all that it should be: let his religious discipline be carefully looked after, according to the Church's plan, by parents and sponsors and pastor, and the question of religious teaching in the school will become comparatively unimportant. The real trouble is, the neglect of religious education out of the school, rather than within it. It is the Godless home, and the indifferent or formal or unspiritual Church, rather than the secular school, that are dwarfing the religious life of this generation.

A candid examination of the history of education, if it were possible within the limits of this inquiry, would go far to explain existing educational questions, and to suggest their solution. It may suffice to point out, that, while for many centuries the direction of education in Europe was almost exclusively in the hands of the Christian clergy, the tendency in modern times has been towards the emancipation of education from ecclesiastical control. In the Church's earliest and best days, the clergy confined themselves to their spiritual functions. For more than two hundred years we have no account of an attempt on their part to control educational work. Their attitude was rather one of helpfulness towards existing institutions of learning, and of a purpose to supplement their work and to evangelize their influence through the Christian nurture of the home and the Church. The time came, however, when the ecclesiastics, especially in the West, began to discredit secular learning as dangerous as well as idle and profane; and, with the irruption of the barbarians, education fell altogether into their hands. A careful study of their conduct of it will disclose the fact, I fear, that their influence was not always favorable to the best results. Undoubtedly, we should not be unmindful of the large debt of gratitude which the world owes to the religious establishments of the dark ages, and especially to a few great monasteries, for keeping alive the torch of learning; but it may be doubted whether, on the whole, the influence of ecclesiasticism upon education was not disastrous. There are few more painful annals than the accounts which have come down to us of the narrow bigotry and even cruelty of the monkish elementary schools, within which children were taught little except a multiplicity of superstitious observances, and learned little except servility of spirit. Under such influences it speedily came to pass, that none but monks and ecclesiastics attained to learned culture at all: the young squires and cadets of energy and promise betaking themselves rather to the castle than to the monastery, to be trained in the presence of gentle ladies and in the ranks of feudal chieftains to deeds of knightliness and feats of arms; while the children of the peasantry and tradesmen grew up in ignorance, content to know no more than to be able to mumble a prayer which they did not understand, or to keep a tally of their daily gains. So it came to pass, that it was unusual for a gentleman to know how to write his name, and this at the time when the wealth and influence of the clergy were greatest, and when they had the education of the people exclusively in their hands. It is perfectly true, that there were eras of progress and improvement, and that the influence of Christianity was then as now altogether favorable to the promotion of human learning. Even mistaken and bigoted monkish methods could not entirely retard the advancement of Christian civilization. Spite of all the blunders of her children, the Church showed herself even then to be the foster-mother of learning; and, under her inspiration, pious founders built and endowed noble universities in different parts of Europe. Nevertheless, it can hardly be denied that elementary education, at least, has been impeded, rather than set forward, by the mastery of ecclesiasticism in the schoolroom. At the Reformation a more notable era of progress than any that had preceded it was begun. In England the clergy, with that wise practical instinct that has generally distinguished them, reformed educational methods in such a way as to keep it largely under their control; yet it cannot be denied, that even there the emancipation of education from ecclesiastical management has gone steadily forward.[1] In Germany emancipation has been pushed to still greater extremes, and under circumstances less favorable to Christianity; while in France ultramontane ecclesiasticism seems to have lost its hold on the control of education altogether. Without taking into consideration the notorious ignorance and degradation of the masses in the Roman-Catholic countries of Southern Europe, where the schools are still in the hands of the Church, it is evident that the exclusive ecclesiastical control of public education has been dis-

---

[1] See a thoughtful article in the Guardian newspaper of Sept. 13, 1882, entitled The Church and the Universities.

credited rather than justified by results. The verdict of history has been against it. The bold and heroic attempt of the Society of Jesus to regain the lost prestige of ecclesiastical direction and government in education has failed in every land; and history is helping us to understand, that however admirable a schoolmaster may now and then be found in the ranks of the clergy, yet it is not a clerical function to teach school, but rather to disciple, to baptize, to teach men to observe the things which Christ commanded.

One disastrous result of the long ecclesiastical domination above referred to yet remains. The monkish teachers of the Middle Ages taught parents to resign the religious education of their children altogether into their hands. In this way, as in numberless ways, the dignity of parental influence and authority was lowered; and parents were encouraged to think that the moral and religious training of their children was a matter of the schoolroom altogether, and not of the Church and of the family. This opinion still prevails. Christian children are often untaught at home. Family religion is often neglected. Parents have not yet returned to their own responsibilities.

The domestic duties of the pastor are often almost wholly undischarged and unknown. This, now, is the dilemma which history has presented to us. Monkish influence first secularized the family or home. Educational progress has now secularized the public school. What is the remedy? I venture to say, that only one remedy is possible. We must revive domestic religion. We must reconsecrate the family to its high and holy office. We must bring the influence of the Church's system of Christian nurture to bear upon the lives of our children. We must bring the influence of Christianity to bear upon secular education in the public schools through the Church and the home.

Practically this is a matter of immense importance. The time has fully come when we must decide what our attitude shall be towards public education. In all the States of this vast country there is to-day a complete system of public schools. No doubt, few of such schools are altogether, or even nearly, what the best friends of education would have them to be. No doubt, many of the methods employed in them are faulty. Yet this system, though a purely con-

ventional one, is now completely established, and
cannot, under existing conditions, be exchanged
for another. And, on the whole, it is a grand system, the very best that could at present, and
when the entire country is considered, be put in
operation. Our public common schools are doing
a grand work. Not only are millions of the children of our own people taught in them, and better
taught than they would be without them, but
other millions of children, born abroad, are welcomed to their hospitable care, emancipated from
traditions and limitations that would otherwise
keep them down, and trained into some degree of
fitness for citizenship in a free State. Here, now,
is a vast and beneficent instrumentality, which we
cannot hope either to supplant or to replace, and
which practically controls the education of this
mighty people. What attitude shall the Church
assume towards it? I say frankly, the Church
should enter cordially and without reserve into
the most intimate possible relations with it, not
only because it is fixed and established, but because as things are, and all things considered, it
is the best general system of education that can
be devised, and because it is capable of being

made still better by the influence which the Church is competent to bring to bear upon it. Let us frankly accept the fact that our common schools are secular; and let us realize, that, so long as they are under State control, it is not only inevitable, but best, that they should be so; and let us bring Christianity to bear upon them in the legitimate and appointed channels of Christian influence. Let us see to it that domestic religion shall be revived, that sponsorship shall become a reality once more, and that our clergy may be pastors indeed of their flocks, feeding and caring for the lambs as well as the sheep. Let us see to it that our children shall go forth in the morning out of the portals of Christian homes, bearing with them the gladness and the peace of Christian nurture; and that, when they return thither, they shall be once more surrounded with all the holy influences of domestic piety. Let their parents and sponsors and pastors bring them up in the nurture and admonition of the Lord, and it will not so much matter if the school to which they go for a few hours each day is altogether secular. If it be asked, What shall be the case of those children who do not live in Christian homes?

the answer is, it is the Church's special work in this world to make their homes Christian. Let the blessed influences of Christianity radiate into all the homes of the land. In this way teachers and parents, as well as children, may be reached. In this way, and along the channels of domestic and social life, the enlightening and ennobling influences of Christianity may be applied to our public schools as well as to the children within them. In this way, at last, our system of popular education may be made Christian in a deeper sense than would necessarily be indicated, even by ecclesiastical direction and control; and so, spite of all disadvantages, we may still realize for this land the old promise, "All thy children shall be taught of the Lord, and great shall be the peace of thy children."

What has hitherto been said has related chiefly to the common or elementary schools of the country. The same principles apply to higher education. We look to the Church and the home to keep watch and ward over our common schools. We look to Christian fathers and mothers and Christian pastors to keep the hearts of the children true, and their feet in the paths of Christian knowledge and peace. The same instrumentalities must be relied on at our institutions of more advanced learning. Around each great university, Christian colleges, halls or homes should be builded, within which the Christian youth of the land might reside while attending the university classes, and over which strong Christian men should preside, not so much to teach religious truth as to fill the lives of the students with a religious spirit. In this land the educational training of the young has been delegated to a system of secular schools and universities. Be it so. Some of these seats of higher learning are nobly planned and completely equipped. Let us frankly and thankfully accept the fact; and let the Church, released as she is from the work of the classroom, betake herself gladly to her own particular function, and build up around each university, and around the lives of her children there, the hallowing, sanctifying influences of Christianity. To do this is not an easy work, but it is the Church's appointed work. Not to teach the *trivium* or *quadrivium*, but to teach men to observe the things which Christ commanded, — this is her appointed work; and she ought to do the latter with all the more energy because she is released from the drudgery of the former. And the Church will do her work all the more effectively when it is once thoroughly realized that Christianity is to be taught, not like a problem of Euclid or an ode of Horace, but through Christian nurture, and by the help of the Spirit of God.

LECTURE V.

CHARITY.

LECTURE V.

CHARITY.

"For ye have the poor with you always, and whensoever ye will ye may do them good." — ST. MARK xiv. 7.

THAT destitution should continue to exist among men has been for ages the *opprobrium* of political economy. All kinds of combinations and arrangements have been proposed, and many of them have been tried, in the vain attempt to banish it from human society. Philosophers have dreamed of model republics, where want should be unknown. Politicians, and tribunes of the people, have proposed and sometimes secured the enactment of agrarian laws, the objects of which were to so limit and distribute property as to provide for the wants of all. Vast colonizing movements have set sail from crowded or inhospitable shores, and have driven their keels into foreign sands, in the hope, that, under fairer or more propitious skies, there should be found such abundance that human indigence should have no place. Malthusian theories, Fourierite plans, and communistic organizations, have been suggested, and sometimes put into operation, to satisfy the obtrusive want that dogs the steps of human progress; but all in vain. The fact of human destitution remains in every land; and we dare not say that it has grown less importunate, or less unwelcome and menacing to the mere economist and civilian, as the world has advanced in civilization. Nor can it be claimed, that the Christian Church has yet propounded a solution of the difficulties by which the State has hitherto been baffled. Both Church and State have elaborated systems for the relief and care of pauperism, which have been worked with a zeal, an intelligence, a devotion, and a wealth of resource, that have left nothing of their kind to be desired. Yet the stubborn fact remains, that the tide of indigent wretchedness does not abate, but is rising, rather, throughout the Christian world.

The methods, whether ecclesiastical or civil, which are here referred to as having been tried without success, may all be designated by the common term, corporate, or institutional, relief.

And however diverse the motives upon which these have rested, yet it is but fair to allow, that, in Christian lands, all of them have been honest attempts to do good to the poor in accordance with Christ's commandment. Before we proceed, then, to consider the causes of their failure, it will be well to inquire what Christ's plan was for dealing with human poverty. We shall then be in a condition to estimate the shortcomings of our human methods, and finally to seek a return to the right way. And the first characteristic of our Lord's attitude towards human poverty, as it seems to me, is, that he frankly recognized the inevitable persistence of it. In his teaching he almost reiterated the precept of the elder law, which said, "The poor shall never cease out of the land: therefore I command thee, saying, Thou shalt open thine hand wide unto thy brother, to thy poor, and to thy needy, in thy land." But Jesus, while he did this, did vastly more. He implicitly declared the presence and the need of the poor to be the perpetual opportunity and the unfailing blessing of his people. More profoundly than the elder law-giver he saw the social and political law on which the fact rested; and he saw, too, how, out of the evil, there might arise abundant good. Yet the optimism of his view did not originate in any sort of indifference to human suffering. Far otherwise. More deeply and tenderly than any other man he was touched with compassion for the poor. More keenly and vividly than any other statesman he realized the anguish of human destitution. More exactly than any other economist, as I trust we shall see, he projected methods for the alleviation of its woes. Nevertheless, he admitted the persistence of it, and based upon this fact many of the most characteristic duties of his system of ethics. It is a fact of deep significance, that Christianity itself, both as taught and exemplified by its Author, was founded on the law of ministry to human need. In order to fulfil this law, he himself came into the world. His whole earthly career may be tersely described by the single phrase, He went about doing good. In sending out his disciples two and two before his face, he charged them with service to the poor. All his ethical teachings took the presence of the poor for granted, and he constantly enjoined ministry to them. To do good, not of abundance merely, but by self-denial; to do good, and lend, hoping for nothing again, — he declared to be the highest human duty, and privilege also; since by so doing, and only so, might men become the children of their Father in heaven. Nay, in one striking passage he identified himself with the poor, and declared that ministry to them, in their hunger and nakedness and squalor and wretchedness, was ministry to him, and entitled to his gratitude and an eternal reward. So completely, then, did he admit the inevitable persistence of poverty, that he adjusted the whole of his ethical system to the treatment of it, and made the proper treatment of it the indispensable condition of his favor, and of access to the joys of heaven.

Acknowledging, then, the persistence of human destitution, he did not seek to banish it from his kingdom. "Ye have the poor with you always." But while he profoundly commiserated their state, and urgently enjoined the duty of ministering to them, he yet enacted that this duty should be wholly voluntary: "Whensoever ye will ye may do them good." He furthermore enacted, that it should be, not only voluntary, but that it should be personal, and performed in a manner altogether unobtrusive, and devoid of publicity; annexing to this personal and secret quality the condition of his approbation. And it is not less notable, that he enjoined the duty of doing good to the poor upon all,—not upon the rich only, but upon the poor also. All are to engage in it, from the beggar to the king; the injunction to do this resting upon the Fatherhood of God and the brotherhood of man. "A new commandment give I unto you, that ye love one another." "Be merciful, as your Father is merciful," "that ye may be the children of your Father which is in heaven."

The mere statement of Christ's attitude towards the poor brings forward some grave and momentous questions, which must be asked, and ought to be answered. Has not civil society assumed an attitude towards the poor, not only different from, but at variance with, that of Christ? And how far has the Church adopted the false attitude of civil society, and abandoned that of the Master? I believe that the charges suggested by these questions are true to a much greater extent than is commonly supposed: and I believe, that in this fact is to be found the secret of that wide-spread alienation between rich and poor, and of the no less wide-spread indifference of both classes to religion, which we all deplore; while to the same cause is to be attributed the growing disaffection of the poorer classes to all civil government, that is one of the most portentous signs of the times. First let us consider the attitude assumed towards the poor by civil society.

Perhaps there is no department of political history more interesting to the statesman than the history of poor-law legislation. Fortunately the sources of information on this subject are abundant and easily accessible. It is not too much to say, that, for more than two and a half centuries, the attention of English economists has been lavished without stint upon this most important subject; while for more than half a century publicists of every Christian nation have been engaged in gathering, arranging, and discussing the statistics of poor-law relief throughout the Christian world. Manifestly, then, not even a sketch of its history can be here attempted; since the bare enumeration of the changes and experiments introduced into the English system alone, would far exceed our limits. It must suffice to say, that poor-law legislation, in our modern sense of the word, began in England, in the reign of Elizabeth, with the Act of 1601, which has been called the "foundation and text-book of English poor law."[1] Before that time, there had been many attempts to deal with destitution by legislative enactment; but the measures devised were rather repressive than remedial, and were so severe and even ferocious as to deserve the name of penal statutes. One of the worst impeachments of mediæval society is found in the cruelty with which crime was punished and the inhumanity with which poverty was repressed by the State down to the period of the Reformation. Previous to that time, the work of poor relief had been undertaken by the Church; vast revenues having been intrusted to her for that purpose. Of the failures and abuses of ecclesiastical charities we must speak presently. With the suppression of many of the religious establishments, and the spoliation of the remainder, the resources which had been employed for the relief of destitution were no longer available; and the question of

[1] Fowle's Poor Law, p. 58.

caring for the needy became in the last degree urgent and menacing. No doubt, the growing spirit of humanity which distinguished the Reformation period moved the brilliant statesmen of the Elizabethan era to attempt some measures of poor relief by law; but it cannot be denied, that the most powerful motives were the selfish desire of the rich to escape from the burden of alms-giving, and the no less selfish purpose of the civilians of that time to pacify the realm, and strengthen the existing order by stilling the importunities of the poor. Of the many mutations of English poor-law we cannot now speak; nor need we dwell on the dreary evidences of failure, that have certainly not diminished to the present time, notwithstanding the immense resources of experience and practical philanthropy that have been brought to bear upon the administration of it. Our own American system of legal relief is mainly a reproduction of the English; though it must be claimed, that our system is, on the whole, better organized, and that, of late years at least, our publicists have availed themselves of a wider study of European methods, and have been able to improve upon the English system in some important particulars. Our American system, however, is so far from being uniform, that it must be described in general terms only. Perhaps it will be sufficient to describe it in general terms as follows: In most, if not in all, of the States of the Union, relief for the destitute is provided by taxation; which relief is administered by commissioners and other officials, under State supervision, chiefly by means of public institutions, such as poorhouses, asylums, and reformatories of a remedial character. No matter what the original cause of the destitution may be, whether it be inherited infirmity, or misfortune, or vice, or improvidence, or incorrigible indolence, the moment a certain condition is reached, the right to public relief is established, and the pauper is entitled to be appropriately cared for under the provisions of the law. Whether the right to such relief can be enforced by an action at law, is a question that has been variously answered: but it cannot be doubted, that the claim of the pauper to his proper relief is a real and substantial one, not to be denied in the court of conscience and at the bar of public opinion;[1]

---

[1] See Fowle's Poor Law, pp. 6, 7.

nor is it easy to see how a refusal to enforce it by a court of law could be justified.

There have been many ingenious attempts to formulate the principle upon which poor-law legislation is founded. One of the most earnest, but most moderate, defenders of the system admits that legal provision for the relief of the destitute seems "artificial and even unnatural; for it establishes a state of things in which persons are not obliged, unless they choose, to provide themselves with the means of subsistence: while those who work for their own living are compelled, whether they like it or not, to maintain those who will not or can not support themselves."[1] That such relief is founded in a natural right to the means of subsistence on the part of the pauper has been widely held: but the consequences of such a principle have been so immediately disastrous and dangerous, that it has been everywhere peremptorily denied; and the denial has been "erected into a maxim of State policy."[2] The other view, that "society is compelled, in the interests of its own self-preservation, to take some care of destitute persons,"[3] can hardly be said to be the "princi-

---

[1] Fowle's Poor Law, p. 1. [2] Ibid. p. 6. [3] Ibid. p. 5.

ple" on which poor-law is founded, though this is gravely insisted on, but reduces legal relief to the category of a mere expedient devised in the interest of selfishness. No doubt, one of the motives of poor-law legislation may be thus defined; but the principle upon which it has proceeded deserves to be placed much higher in the scale of merit. A candid examination of poor-law history will prove, I think, that legal relief is an attempt to obey the injunction of Christ and the dictates of Christian humanity by making a sure and certain provision for human destitution. That the attempt has been a failure, I am going to try to show. It is also undeniable, I think, that the motive which has prompted this attempt has been largely mixed with selfishness. Relief by law has been adopted as a cheap and easy expedient. To quote once more from the author above referred to, even so zealous a defender of the English poor-law system, while he does not admit the truth of the charge, that it is "due neither to humanity nor genuine utilitarianism, but to the interests of mere class selfishness," does admit, that "the true statement of the case would seem to be, that the selfishness of the upper classes took advantage of the growing spirit of humanity, and made a kind of tacit bargain with it."[1] Nevertheless, the principle upon which poor-law legislation has always really proceeded, is the principle, as I have said, of administering charity by law.

That poor-law legislation has failed to attain its object, or, in other words, that legal relief of destitution has been, not only ineffective, but actually disastrous to the best interests of human benevolence and of human well-being, seems to me to be shown by the following considerations. In the first place, as a charitable instrumentality, legal relief defeats itself at the outset; since charity by law is impossible, being a contradiction of terms. The moment relief ceases to be personal and voluntary, it ceases to be charity. Nor is this all. It defeats itself in another notable particular. In order to entitle a person to become a beneficiary of legal relief, all that is necessary is, that he should be reduced by misfortune, improvidence, or vice to a state of indigence. But the moment he sinks to this condition, and accepts the provision made for it by law, he becomes a pauper.

[1] Fowle's Poor Law, p. 14.

While he was simply a needy person, and before he availed himself of the legal bounty arranged for his relief, he was simply one of the poor. The moment after he accepted such relief, he became a pauper. There is a distinction, then, between pauperism and poverty; and it is the characteristic of the poor-law, that it created pauperism, and thrust it in poverty's place. But the pauper is not any longer a poor man. He has a property in the public provision arranged for his support. He has a right, as we have seen, to the bounty set apart for him by taxation. We are entitled to remark, then, that the poor-law system completely misses the object for which it was created. It undertook to provide for the poor man; and, behold, it has converted him into a pauper with a property in the provision made for him. Now, whether we conclude that this is a benefit, or the reverse, — that this transformation from poverty to pauperism is an elevation or a degradation, — certain it is that the effect of the poor-law takes relief altogether out of the category of charity. It is simply a question of legal duty on the one side, and of lawful right on the other. The expedient of legal relief, then, has failed, as an agency for administering charity to the poor.

But, further, the creation of pauperism has not only failed in this respect, but it has proved vastly hurtful to the interests of benevolence. The wants of poverty are not as well cared for, the needs of destitution are not as well ministered to, as they would be if this device of civil society were altogether swept away. The reason is, that, because society has adopted this artificial and mistaken method, there are certain natural channels of supply that are seriously obstructed. And, first, the degrading and disabling effect of the poor-laws upon the poor themselves is to be noted. The strongest instinct of our nature is the instinct of self-preservation. With many necessity is the only motive-power masterful enough to get things done. The instinct of self-preservation, if rightly developed, will lead men to look to the future; and there are multitudes of those who live and must live near the borderland of want who can be induced to look ahead, and provide for the future, by no less urgent and inexorable law. Now, it is a fact, that, among such classes, improvidence is the rule; and it is more than a mere economic evil.

It means self-indulgence and selfishness, instead of self-control and self-sacrifice. It means riotous living; as all wasting of one's substance, be it much or little, is: and this is induced by the unconscious feeling which poor-laws are precisely fitted to produce. The process is not often conscious nor always logical. The feeling is, that the worst is provided for, — that want, absolute want, cannot befall. The truculent saying, that the world owes every man a living, seems to be registered in a law of the land; and we cannot wonder that it finds an echo in many a poor man's heart and life, encouraging him to live up to his means, and to be improvident. And let it not be forgotten, that the thought of pauperism, which is so dreadful to a man of competent means, is by no means so shocking to or remote from multitudes of those who live on the very verge of penury. Our poor-laws have done much to make such thoughts possible and not unwelcome. The county-house with its imposing exterior, the machinery of the administration of legal relief, the right to such relief which the law confers, — all these have tended to break the horror of the fall; so that it is not too much to say, that, of the multitudes who find their way to our county-houses, not a few have been drawn thither by a kind of baleful and malefic attraction. This, then, is a grave charge against our whole system of legal relief, quite apart from any faults connected with the administration of it, that the very promise of such relief has created a demand for it by breaking down the self-reliance, the foresight, the moral strength, of the poor.

Another source of bounty to the poor that legal relief has largely impaired, is the natural obligation and impulse that move the near relations of the helpless poor to take care of them. Perhaps the most detestable and alarming result of the poor-laws is the loosening of natural ties, the weakening of the bonds of natural affection, the release of families from the obligation to take care of their own poor. If the facts could be accurately ascertained, a diseased condition of the lower ranks of the body politic in this respect would be disclosed that would be absolutely appalling. The aged poor are relegated to the poorhouse by unnatural sons and daughters all over the land. Among the poorer classes the disgrace of it is often not felt. It is easy to plead that it is not wrong to accept a provision which is a legal right. And the wrong is not done merely to the aged father and mother, who are often more than willing to escape to the peace of the poorhouse; but the wrong is done also to the children, who thus lose their parents in the worst sense, to their home, to their own lives, and their own souls, and to the lives and souls of their children. Happy the home beside whose portal the aged sit in the calm peace of declining years, while their sons and daughters gain dignity and honor from God and man as they pay back in some degree the debt of love and reverence which they owe to parental care! and woe to the homes, the children, and the land where the aged no longer sit in the doors of the poor! And that this woe is stealing over our land is not more evident than that it is largely due to the relaxation of family obligations which our poor-laws have partly brought about. The very fact that he knows legal provision to have been made, and that absolute want cannot visit those belonging to him, is sufficient in multitudes of cases to set the truant husband, the unnatural child, the selfish brother, free from the slight bond that would otherwise hold him to duty; and so large numbers of those whom natural affection ought to care for are consigned to the bounty of public relief. And, in doing this, the home and the family life of the poor are being desecrated. The most sacred and humanizing of all the natural affections are neutralized among those who need them most. Selfishness is working its deadly alienations in the dwellings of the poor.

In the next place, the legal provision that has been made for the relief of penury has had a chilling and paralyzing effect upon the bounty and charity of the rich. The poor-laws are a welcome and favorite device of the independent classes, who are often not loath to believe in the sufficiency of their own method. Moreover, the effect of the poor-law is, to exile the paupers, and still their importunity. But, above all, it has changed the attitude of the poor themselves from the gentle and amiable attitude of exigence and gratitude to the truculent attitude of demand and resentment.[1] The result is disastrous in the last degree, not only to the poor, but to the rich as well. I think it is capable of being demonstrated,

[1] Fowle's Poor Law, p. 13.

that, if the poor were left to the voluntary care of their more fortunate neighbors, there would be no lack of abundant means to provide for their real necessities. But the matter of providing for the poor is not wholly nor even chiefly a question of money. The rich have something vastly more precious and helpful than money, which they ought to give, but which, under our present system, is too often not given; and that is, personal sympathy, personal interest, personal friendliness and good will, to be manifested, as they can only be manifested, in the frank and unrestricted intercourse between rich and poor. One of the evil results of our present system is, that the poor are largely bereaved of the personal sympathy of the rich. And not less is the loss to the rich themselves. They are deprived of the gratitude, the friendship, the friendliness, of the poor. The softening, elevating influence of benefactorship is taken from them. Princely though their gifts may be, and large their charities, yet these go through legal or institutional channels too often, and meet no return of thanks, or of gratitude even: such givers never hear the sweetest music that ever greets human ears, — the music of the benediction of the poor. Not merely, then, for the sake of the poor, but for the sake of the rich also, we ought to plead and pray for the old method of charity by love instead of charity by law. Verily, it is always and everywhere hard for the rich man to enter into the kingdom of heaven; but by pauperizing the poor, and banishing them in their unloveliness and squalor, we have made it harder still for the rich to win the plaudit of the Master, "Inasmuch as ye have done it unto one of the least of these my brethren, ye have done it unto me."

But there is another resource of helpfulness to the poor, which is vaster and more important than any that I have yet named; and this, too, is obstructed and impaired by our present system. I mean the sympathy and helpfulness which the poor would extend to each other if left to the natural promptings of benevolence and charity. The most precious of all the gifts of sympathy and help that ever come to the poor man in his distress are the heartfelt sympathy and help of his neighbors, of those who live around his dwelling. The nameless and numberless sweet charities of neighborliness that come in the natural order of things, unbidden, from those who live hard by, — these are the sweetest and most helpful of all benefactions. They not only cheer and gladden the poor man's lot, but they teach him self-respect and self-help as nothing else can. And it is, perhaps, the worst impeachment of our legal system, that it has done much — far more than most of us are aware of — to dry up these sources of consolation. He who studies the condition of the indigent classes is struck by the lack of brotherly kindness among them. There may be guilds and sodalities and combinations among them; but these result from community of opinion or interest, and not from mere propinquity, mere neighborhood, and neighborliness. We have seen how, in the multitude that live on the verge of want, our system has relaxed the bonds of family affection. It has had the same effect in preventing the interchange of charity among the poor. And, in drying up this source of help and comfort, the lives of our poor are doubly impoverished and doubly desolated. The poor man is bereaved of the help of his neighbor, and of the opportunity to help his neighbor. The virtue and the grace of helpfulness, of sympathy, of charity, have been made difficult, and sometimes almost impossible, to him.

But not alone to the rich and the poor as classes, but to civil society as a whole, the result of our system of legal relief has been most disastrous. The increasing alienation between the two ranks of society is largely due to the causes here suggested. The natural bond between the rich and the poor has been sundered. The natural law which binds them together has been in large degree set aside. We do not often think, perhaps, how indispensable a factor poverty is in civilization and progress. It is hardly too much to say, if there was no poverty, there could be no wealth. Certainly, without poverty wealth would be of little value. It is no depreciation of the dignity of even the humblest labor to say, that the more menial and unwelcome offices of life would never be done by one man for another unless the need of the one and the affluence of the other brought it about. If there were no poor, every man would have to do these offices for himself; and there could be no large administrations of business or commerce, no domestic elegance, no learned leisure, no patronage of art. Indeed, in the true sense of the word, there could be no rich if there were no poor. The poor, then, are quite as indispensable to the rich, to say the least, as the rich are to the poor. Their fortunes should be bound up together. It is an unnatural and an evil condition that separates them and antagonizes them instead of making them the friends that they ought to be; and, whenever this alienation takes place, the rift has begun, which, slowly widening, must throw civil society at last into chaos. To the question, then, What shall be done to avert this, the most alarming evil of our times, and bring the rich and poor together again? there is but one answer. It is not by legal or mechanical relief that it can be done, no matter how bountiful. It is not by the diffusion of intelligence merely. It is not by external force. It must be done by flinging all classes, rich and poor alike, back on the old law of mutual helpfulness and sympathy; by discontinuing charity by law, and relying on the charity of love.

These arguments are sufficiently cogent, it seems to me, from the stand-point of our common humanity. Their urgency is immeasurably increased when we come to consider them from the stand-point of the Christian. Our present system of legal relief is a grievous wrong to the Church and the cause of Christianity. By substituting charity by law for the charity of love, we have deprived the Church, in some measure at least, of her noblest work, of her most precious opportunity. Far more precious, not only to those to whom she ministers, but also to herself and her ministering servants, than any ministry of truth and light, is her ministry of love. To minister to human want and human sorrow, — this is her privilege and her mission. Bereave her of this, and you rob her of her most precious power. It is in exercising her ministry to human need that she realizes her mastery, and her only real mastery, over the souls of men. Only so, — not otherwise. It is not till the rich man feels his need, that the Church can reach and minister to him. No more can she reach the poor man, unless she offers ministry to his need also. Failure to do this, is the reason why so many churches are unfilled by the poor. It is not because the poor feel out of place. It is not because they prefer to company with one another. It is because the one, only appeal that can reach them is not made; and that is, the appeal of personal sympathy and love. It is not by preaching merely; it is not by music merely; it is not by ritual or the absence of it; it is not by mechanical guilds and unions merely, nor sham tea-drinkings and sociables: it can be done only in the old way in which Christ did it, and commissioned his Church to do it; that is, by going about doing good; by carrying the gospel and sweet human sympathy and friendliness into the homes, the hiding-places, of the poor. And this brings us to say, that neither has the Church been altogether blameless in this matter. For a long time the Church has been inclined to adopt wholesale expedients, to rely largely on official methods, and to substitute institutional charity for the old-fashioned personal charity of love.

The study of religious institutional charity is full of profoundest interest. It had its origin in ecclesiastical monasticism, and owes its development to the conditions which in turn acted on the monastic life, and were created by it. Time does not permit me to more than sketch its history. The cenobitic, or monastic, life does not owe its origin to Christianity. It sprang out of certain natural impulses of human nature, and had existed for centuries in the East, and for a long time among the Jews before the coming of Christ. Under the stress of heathen persecution, however, the early Christians, partly by the accident of exile, and partly by choice, were led to seek refuge in its seclusion; and it soon came to pass, that the *lauri* of the Thebaid and the caves of Syria were filled with Christian hermits, who devoted themselves to a contemplative life. Under the influence of Antony, — a noble Egyptian, — and other like-minded men, something like order and organization began to grow up among these scattered recluses, until, by reason of the patronage and example of the pious and well-born, monasticism became thoroughly established. The political and social condition of Western Christendom after the irruption of the barbarians rendered monastic institutions peculiarly useful. They were the only asylums for a long time wherein the defenceless and oppressed could find a refuge from the cruelty and rapacity of robber chieftains and feudal despots. Within their quiet and peaceful shades, moreover, learning was kept alive; and the gentler arts of peace survived in an age which would otherwise have crushed them by force of arms. Beyond all question, the cause of learning and of humanity owes a large debt of gratitude to the monks of the Middle Ages, and to their monasteries and schools. Yet the good that they did was not unmixed with evil. It has been pointed out with much force, that they did vast evil in withdrawing the nobler natures, the gentler spirits, the real heroes of love and self-sacrifice, from society and from the economies of life, and leaving the race to be propagated, and its practical destinies to be shaped, by the selfish, the fierce, the brutal, the cruel. Not less disastrous was the effect of the withdrawal of the sweet charities of the gospel from the homes and the home-life of the people, and the transfer of these charities to the wicket of the monastery gate, to the cloister of the nunnery, to the asylum, and the orphanage. A celibate and monkish clergy, and cenobitic sisterhoods, in withdrawing from the homes of the people, discontinued the pastoral office, recalled the ministries of religion and charity from the fireside, abandoned the dwellings of the people to barbarism, degraded the family, and substituted the devotions of the oratory and the cell for family religion and domestic piety. The result was, that institutional charity took the place, to a large extent, of the charity of house to house visitation, of personal and pastoral care, and of neighborly brotherly love. So vast did the evils of the system grow, that reformation after reformation became absolutely necessary; and, in England especially, the strong arm of the law had to be interposed again and again, to limit, to regulate, and to control such charities. Certain it is, that the evils of their internal administration were enormous; and no less evil was their influence on many of their beneficiaries. The dole at the monastery gate was quite as efficacious as the relief of the modern "poor-master" in degrading and pauperizing the poor.

The day of monasticism is over, at least in Western Christendom. No effort and no combination can ever restore it to its old place of influence. Nevertheless, the evil of it is not eradicated, but survives in many forms. The poor-laws are themselves a modification of it; the object being, to transfer the administration of charity from the chapter-house to the county-board, — to substitute the relief of law for the dole of the monastery wicket. Moreover, it survives in the institutional charity of the Roman-Catholic Church, and in the tendency of all religious bodies to merge their charities in the same institutionalism. A careful study of the Roman-Catholic system, and of the condition of the Roman-Catholic poor, would bring some significant facts to light. It would be seen, I venture to assert, that, under that system, the domestic life of the Roman-Catholic poor is largely uncared for; that family religion is almost unknown among them; that their homes are, to a large extent, unvisited and neglected. If one is sick, there is the hospital; if one is orphaned, there is the orphanage; if one is destitute and old, there is the retreat: but home is not the sanctuary nor the refuge; home is stripped of its sacredness, and the charitable institution is exalted and glorified. The effect of all this is seen in the fact, that, in those communities composed partly of Roman Catholics and partly of Protestants, by far the largest part of the destitution belongs to the former. And this destitution is often outcast and vicious, hiding in slums, breeding paupers and criminals. Pastoral work, in the true sense of the word, is rare among the Roman-Catholic clergy, as is natural with a priesthood who have no family ties, and know little or nothing of domestic life; and personal charity is swallowed up, to a large extent, by institutional charity. I would not detract aught from the praise that is due to the self-denying and self-sacrificing orders and sisterhoods of that communion. I do not deny that much good is done through their many institutions and instrumentalities of charitable work. I only say, that these last have been far from an unmixed good. In so far as they have overshadowed the family and home life, withdrawn the ministries of religion from the dwellings of the people, and substituted a charity of system for a charity of personal love, they have occasioned enormous evil. They have paralyzed the choicest agency that the Christian Church can use in winning the hearts of the poor, and correcting the selfishness of the rich. It is the shadow of the monastery that blights and withers the home-life of Italy and Spain; and institutionalism constitutes the weakness, and not the strength, of Romanism in America to-day.

But the evil is not confined to Romanism. Among all religious bodies, there is a tendency to confide to religious organizations and institutions what ought to be done by personal charity. Extreme Protestants have been disposed to follow the impulse of that Puritanism and independency of which we have already spoken, and to make the administration of charity a political affair, or a mere department of the State. Roman Catholics have tended, for a different reason, as we have seen, to confide it to ecclesiastical machinery. It remains for us, if we will, to adopt as ours the gospel plan, and, in working it wisely and unweariedly, to win for our heritage the poor of this land. But, before we proceed to consider the function of Christianity in this behalf, let us first inquire how Christianity and civil society are related in the administration of charity.

Recurring to the philosophic idea of civil society, it is easy to see that the State will have such authority and power in the matter of caring for the destitute as are delegated to it, and no more. The State, as such, is under no inherent or paternal obligation to care for indigence. Poor-laws are simply a political arrangement, a civic device, whereby the body politic agrees to place a certain sum, raised by taxation, in the public treasury, and to employ the civic authorities to apply and administer the same. It may be granted, that such power and authority may be properly delegated to the State. Granting this, however, one or two important conclusions arise, which have already been indicated, one of which may here be stated again. That is, that, whatever this provision may be, it is not charity. Whatever obligation rests upon a man to be charitable cannot be discharged, in whole or in part, in this way. For charity, however deliberate and prudent, must be both personal and voluntary. It must be the voluntary expression of an inward affection. It must be a pure and unqualified gift, or it is not charity. But relief provided by legal enactment cannot be this. The beneficiary has a right to it: it is his property. Legal relief, then, is not charity at all, and, from the nature of the case, cannot be. That it is not wise and efficacious has already been demonstrated, but the effort to make it efficacious has arisen out of a natural impulse of our common humanity. Christ took this impulse, and transformed it. He spiritualized it, transmuting pity into charity. He took it into his service, confiding to it the lofty mission of healing the sicknesses, consoling the sorrows, and ministering to the destitution, of the human race. And, as knowing that a grace so tender and so divine could not exist in an atmosphere of selfishness or officialism, he charged his disciples, saying, "Take heed that ye do not your alms before men, to be seen of them." "But when thou doest alms, let not thy left hand know what thy right hand doeth: that thine alms may be in secret: and thy Father which seeth in secret himself shall reward thee openly." In a word, he delegated this ministry to the personal and pastoral care of his servants and handmaids, and exemplified it in his own life of benediction and benefaction in the homes of the poor.

Let us try, then, to understand that Christian charity cannot be made a matter of legal enactment at all. The attempt to do so has been disastrous to poor and rich alike. It belongs to the Church, according to Christ's appointment, to minister wisely and tenderly to the poor. This brings forward certain practical questions which demand our consideration. First, it will be asked, shall our poor-laws be at once repealed, and our poorhouses shut up? Since legal relief does not accomplish all that is desired, shall it be at once abandoned? To this I answer, that, so far as mere resources are concerned, the poor-laws might, if practicable, be at once repealed. In a short time private charity could be relied on to supply more than would thus be given up. Nevertheless, to seek the repeal at once, or under existing conditions, of so mature a system, is not to be thought of. What remains to be done is, to make it more and more unnecessary and superfluous. This, I think, is a work which we Christians ought to propose to ourselves, and ever keep in view; and this we can do only by taking such care of the poor, according to Christ's plan, that there shall be no paupers left in the land.

But in the next place, in the doing of this, and in order to this, we must reconstruct to a great extent our charitable methods. Not only must charity be personal and voluntary, but it must be made to do the poor good. And this is to be accomplished, only by the manifold ministries of brotherly love. Unless the giving of money, then, shall do the poor good, it is not charity to give it. If it shall do them harm, we dare not give it. But, even when it is good to give, much, and sometimes all the good, depends on the manner of giving. "Give alms of thy goods" is only a part of the precept: the second is no less imperative and not less important, — "Never turn thy face from any poor man." Personal sympathy, personal helpfulness, counsel, encouragement, employment, the teaching of self-control, self-respect, self-reliance, in their homes, in their families, by their firesides, — these are the ministries of charity; and these must be accompanied by the highest of all the ministries of love, or, rather, they must be made a part of the ministry of the gospel to the poor.

What shall be done, then, with our institutional charity? To this I answer, let us keep it up bravely, let us sustain it bountifully, let us administer it wisely as long as it is necessary, but let us outgrow it as soon as we can. Doubtless, there will always be need of some charitable institutions; but it ought to be a decreasing need. The more thoroughly we do our work in the homes and hearts of the poor, the less will such need be. The orphanage is, indeed, a blessed charity; but more blessed is the state of that people whose orphans find Christian homes with relatives and neighbors. A home for the aged is a beautiful charity; but far more beautiful is it to see the old sitting by the door or fireside of their children or grandchildren, and lending the benediction of their presence to the homes of the poor. So also with more heroic institutions. It is a blessed thing to have a reform school, for instance, to which to send a bad boy; but how much better it would be to so surround that poor boy's cradle and home with good influences, that he might be a good boy instead of a bad one. Reform schools are filled by the neglect of Christian people just as our poorhouses are filled. Christianity should propose to itself this end, to supersede all these institutions, whether civil or ecclesiastical. They are not the glory of a land. They are a reproach rather. And when we begin to feel this, and cease from our easy and self-sufficient pride in these things, we may hope to return to Christ's method of caring for the poor.

To do this is the Church's present opportunity. It is along this line, as I believe, that she may win the masses, strengthen the State, and become the Church of this people. No doubt, the way is long and arduous; but it is the way which Christ pointed out, and there is no other. Howbeit, we cannot hope to walk in it except we be endued with power from on high. There must be a revival of the true pastoral office among the clergy. There must be a genuine revival of brotherly love. There is no need of asking or waiting for the enactments of conventions and synods and councils. Such a movement cannot be set in operation by legislation. Let each pastor and congregation simply return to Christ's ways, and go to work! Let us first accept the Master's saying, that the poor are to be with us always; and then let us seek to gain and to learn from the Spirit the will and the way to do them good.

LECTURE VI.

THE ULTIMATE ISSUE.

LECTURE VI.

THE ULTIMATE ISSUE.

"Pilate therefore said unto him, Art thou a king then? Jesus answered, Thou sayest that I am a king. To this end was I born, and for this cause came I into the world, that I should bear witness unto the truth. Every one that is of the truth heareth my voice." — ST. JOHN xviii. 37.

IN this passage we are told how the particular issue which is now to engage our thought, and with the consideration of which this series of lectures is to end, was raised in the trial of our Lord. He had just repudiated once more, and in terms, all claim to temporal sovereignty. He had just declared, in the most solemn manner, that his kingdom was not of this world. But, as has been well pointed out, the words in which this renunciation was made, "not only deny; they affirm; if not of this world, then of another world. They assert this other world before the representative of those who boasted of their '*orbis terrarum.*'"[1] It was this implied claim to another kingdom that led to

---

[1] Alford, *in loc.*

Pilate's further question, in which, with disguised impatience and sarcasm, he asked, "Art thou a king then?" Nevertheless, Pilate's question was not altogether sarcastic. He must have had some dim sense of the meaning that lay hid in the reserve of Jesus. He must have dimly felt that a new and strange conjuncture had been arrived at in the political history of the world, when, at the bar of the imperial power, there stood one who, though unarmed and defenceless, and who, though he repudiated earthly royalty, yet claimed, nevertheless, to be a king. Strange claim, and startling, too, in that cruel, haughty presence, and within that martial hall! Strange and startling to the Cæsar's representative, to hear that there was a kingdom which rested on something else than the might of arms; which could exist without measuring swords with Roman legionaries; which earthly pomp could not overawe, and earthly power could not take away. "Art thou a king then?" It raised the question which state-craft has ever since been propounding; too often unheeding, as Pilate did, the wonderful answer of Jesus, "Thou sayest that I am a king. To this end was I born, and for this cause came I into the world, that I should bear witness unto the truth. Every one that is of the truth heareth my voice."

The kingdom which Jesus repudiated is here set over against the kingdom which he claimed. It will be instructive to contrast the one with the other. We have seen that the first, as represented by the imperial procurator, based its pretension to authority upon a certain divine right. Nevertheless, in the thought of Jesus, its true authority, as we have also seen, rested simply on the consent, or, if you please, the submission, of the governed. The first contrast, then, between the kingdom repudiated by Jesus, and that claimed by him, which challenges our attention, arises out of the fact, that the one was from beneath, the other from above; the one was merely secular and civil, the other was theocratic and spiritual; the one was of this world, the other was not of this world. The distinction heretofore pointed out between the Church as a theocracy, and the State as a political and civil arrangement, which, however authoritative, yet derives its authority from human consent, was obviously present to the mind of Jesus. He pointed out, that the two kingdoms are not only not identical, but that they cannot be; that they are incompatible, since they rest on principles wholly different. He not only asserted that his kingdom was not of this world, but he proceeded to show that it could not be, by further indicating the nature of his own royalty. And, in doing this, he spoke as one having inherent authority; as one who was born for the purpose of exercising this dominion; as one who came into the world to be a king. This, then, is the fundamental distinction between Church and State, between Christianity and civil society. The one is theocratic: the other is democratic, or popular. The one derives its real authority from beneath: the other, from above. The one is of this world: the other is not of this world.

The next obvious point of contrast is found in the difference between the objects which are to be served by the two kingdoms. The object of the one is the maintenance of external order. The object of the other is the establishment of truth. The one has to do with those matters of expediency and propriety which are committed to it. The other has to do with the eternal things which concern the souls of men, and which each soul must face and deal with in his own personality. By implication it is here declared, that with this latter function the kingdoms of this world have nothing whatever to do. In the peculiar claim which Jesus here made to exclusive dominion in the realm of truth, he declared that the State has no right or authority over conscience. Not more distinctly did he himself repudiate the sword of secular power than he denied the right of the State to wield the sword of spiritual power; and, in making this distinction, he enacted the real separateness of Church and State, not only renouncing in terms the right of the Church to control or even interfere in things political, but also declaring, by necessary implication, that the dominion of the State does not rightly include the realm of conscience and the domain of truth. Could the distinction thus made have been always preserved in Christian thought, it is easy to see how the numberless evils of Byzantinism and the Papacy could never have arisen; how almost all the strifes and contentions which have disgraced Christian history might have been avoided; and how the real royalty of Christ might long since have been acknowledged, even in this world: for it is only by keeping steadily in view his own renunciation of temporal sovereignty, that we can realize his true sovereignty, and understand the breadth and the depth and the height of his own saying, that all power has been given to him, both in heaven and in earth.

To the capital question, then, How is the doctrine of the secular sovereignty of the State to be reconciled with the assertion of the divine royalty of Christ? our Lord himself has supplied the answer. The two occupy different spheres, and rest on different bases of authority. The answer which he made at the bar of Pilate's judgment-hall was at once a complete assertion of his own kingship, and a complete vindication of himself from the charge of interfering with the proper function of the State. In other words, our Lord himself, in allowing the secular sovereignty of the State, and asserting his own divine royalty, declared that the two were not contradictory; and the iniquity of Pilate's condemnation of him, which has been well called the most profligate crime in history, lies in the fact, that though he admitted the completeness of the answer of Jesus, and acknowledged, that, in making himself a king, he was not speaking against Cæsar, yet he weakly yielded to the clamor of the Jews, and condemned him, in whom he found no fault at all, to death. Let us, then, once more accept the definition of our Lord himself, so solemnly made in the supreme moment of his arraignment and trial, of the difference between his kingdom and the kingdoms of this world. Let us not refuse to adopt the discrimination which he so clearly made between the authority of the one as resting on his divine mission, and the authority of the other as resting on the consent or submission of the people. Let us acknowledge with him, that the one is altogether theocratic, and the other wholly secular; and that, while the sphere of the one is the domain of truth, the sphere of the other is civil and social order. The question remains, What effect does the enlarging and deepening of Christ's kingdom have upon the stability and authority of civil society?

In the first place, Christianity re-enforces the social impulse in which civil society originates, and which operates to hold it together. As man is by nature a "political being;" so Christianity strengthens the natural social appetency, not only by removing or breaking down the hinderances of it, but by adding to it the strong motive-power of brotherly love. I need not stay to prove that Christ first proclaimed the brotherhood of man, and based upon it the new commandment, that men should love one another; that brotherly love is one of the characteristic graces of the Christian life;[1] and that such charity or brotherly love can nowhere be found but under the influence and administration of the Spirit of God. Now, the operation of this new force in human history is nowhere so conspicuous as in the effect it has upon civil society. Selfishness, which is the very elemental cause of all social disorder, is attacked in its citadel, the human heart. All the disorderly vices, such as lust, violence, perfidy, are assailed by Christianity at their source. The love which works no ill to his neighbor, and is the fulfilling of the law, is supplied by Christianity to maintain and uphold social order at every point; and, as an added motive, this characteristic affection of Christianity draws the bonds of civil society more closely together. The social compact becomes something more than a mere civil arrangement: it rests on something more than a merely natural

---

[1] Rom. xii. 10; 1 Thess. iv. 9; Heb. xiii. 1.

"*appetitus societatis.*" It is re-enforced by an impulse of brotherly affection, which not only works no ill to his neighbor, but which seeks by combination and intercourse to do him good. In becoming a Christian, then, a man is made a better citizen; and the State, whatever its form may be, has its true basis of authority strengthened by the Christianization of its people.

But not only does Christianity re-enforce the social and political appetency upon which civil society is founded, but it also exalts and dignifies it. A new sanction is added to the obligation of it, in discovering to man his true dignity and destiny. In disclosing to the soul its relation to God, in bringing life and immortality to light, the transcendental truth is brought home to man, that he is more than a mere "political animal;" that his true life is the life of his undying spirit; and that all things which affect him here are to be measured and valued accordingly as they affect his spiritual well-being. And, in doing this, all his social impulses are ennobled, as well as made more cogent and authoritative. Man lives best in this world by living for another and a higher. The man lives to most purpose here whose life here is felt by him to be a training for immortality. It is one of those profound truths peculiar to and characteristic of the gospel, that it is not by living for this world, but by living above it; that it is not by fixing our regard on this lower life, but by losing it in our regard to a higher; that it is not by seeking first and supremely the things of this world, but rather by seeking first the kingdom of God and his righteousness, — that man's noblest destiny, even in this life, is to be attained. And not only does Christianity ennoble man by thus enlarging his horizon, but it also supplies him with the only energy which is adequate to enable him to realize his highest destiny, both hereafter and here. In a noble passage in the "Republic" of Plato, the Platonic Socrates is made to say of the man of understanding, that he will look at the city within him, and will regulate his life according to the ideals which are discernible there. "In heaven," he says, "there is laid up a pattern of such a city; and he who desires may behold this, and, beholding, govern himself accordingly."[1] Nevertheless, the Platonic philosophy discovered no motive-

[1] Republic, bk. ix.

power sufficient to enable man to realize the heavenly ideals to which it pointed him; nor have other philosophers been more successful in their search for some moral energy with which to enable and hold to its allegiance the frail and wandering heart. Christianity alone has done this, in supplying to man, not only a divine Ideal to love, to imitate, to worship, but also a divine Energy, even the Holy Spirit, to guide and to inspire those who love the Lord Jesus, and to enable them to have his mind, to yield to his will, and to feel, and repeat in compassionate tenderness for others, the beatings of his loving heart. Fashioned according to this Ideal, the man becomes a true lover of his country, because a true lover of his kind. His spiritual affections and appetences are all engaged on the side of civic peace and social order. Unearthly motives are added to those of this lower life. The man is himself transformed: and all the impulses upon which civil society rests are strengthened, ennobled, and exalted at their source; that is to say, in the individual conscience and the individual heart.

Here, then, is the kingdom of Jesus. While, in the nature of the case, it does not, and can not when rightly considered, interfere with the kingdoms of this world, it deals with the deep foundations upon which the kingdoms of this world must rest. Christianity, then, is related to civil society as a supernatural operation, a divine influence affecting the individual man. This is the sole legitimate sphere of the influence of religion in politics. It does not rightly deal with government as such. It rightly claims no authority over the State, and rightly seeks no alliance with it. It does not rightly undertake to deal with men in the mass, but with the individual soul. But, within this domain, Jesus the King is shaping the destiny of the world. And it is to be observed, that it has been only thus; that it has been only by working in this way from the individual and with him; that it has been only by maintaining this one point of relation, and operating through this one point of contact, between Christianity and civil society, — that Jesus has actually exercised in human history the royalty which he claimed for himself. Not otherwise has he wielded the sceptre of his kingly power on earth. Not otherwise has he undertaken to shape the earthly destiny of man. But within this sphere, in the realm of conscience, in the wide domain of spiritual or eternal truth, in the unseen courts of the soul, he has made his power felt; and thus he has shown, in a far deeper sense than any earthly sovereignty could indicate, that all power has indeed been given to him in heaven and in earth.

It is well seen, in the light of these considerations, how entirely salutary the effect of true Christianity must be upon civil and social order. While, undoubtedly, the tendency of Christian influence has been to secularize the State, and thus reduce it to its true place, yet it is not and can not be rightly in conflict with it. On the contrary, as we have seen, it re-enforces its true authority, and also adds to its real power over the conduct of men. Hence, though Christianity, working in its proper sphere, has undoubtedly discredited despotism, and gone far to banish it from the earth; yet it has strengthened rather than weakened the true and proper authority of the State. And this it must do more and more if left free to work in its proper sphere. All its appropriate and essential influences tend towards the upbuilding and strengthening of civil society. In our own land, where the true basis of civil society is recognized, and where the Church is emancipated from State interference and State control, the service done to civil and social order by Christianity is incalculable. And this service is great and salutary because it is rendered in the proper domain of Christian influence, not to the State as such, and not to the people through the State, but to the souls of the men who constitute the State; thus applying its benign and wholesome influence to the very sources of political authority. Nor is it to be forgotten, that the service which religion renders to the State is not less, but is really greater and more salutary, because it is directed, not to man's temporal, but to his eternal, well-being, not to his political, but to his spiritual, good. Certainly, we need not look beyond the borders of our own land to see the truth signally exemplified, that civil and social order has no friend more serviceable than the Christian preacher and pastor who devotes himself to the duties of his sacred office, refusing to intermeddle with political questions; while here as everywhere the political priest, the partisan preacher, is a disquieter of public peace, a disturber of civil society. In other words, Christianity is serviceable to the State when it is neither obtruded nor drafted into the service of the State, but is left free to work in its own sphere, with its own agencies, and for its own proper ends. The moment it is thrust out of its own proper domain, and made to do duty as a political instrumentality, its dignity is debased, its beneficence is abolished. And the reason of this lies in the nature of things. For the proper spheres of religion and politics are essentially different. Political Christianity is a contradiction of terms. Christianity abdicates its high function, and lays aside its crown, when it enters the arena of political strife. Nay, more, it then becomes an instrument of enormous evil. It is not at all strange, that the very worst political despotisms have been the despotisms of ecclesiastical ministries and cabals, and that the weakest and most unworthy rulers of the world have been priest-ridden kings. For Christianity, degraded or perverted into the service of this world, is found to be unfit to do even this world service. It is like a fallen angel, which, ceasing to be the messenger of unearthly good, becomes the instrument of unearthly evil.

The same limitation, arising out of the very

nature of things, renders it impossible for the State to wisely and beneficently interfere with religion. Large as is the debt of gratitude which civil society owes to Christianity, it cannot recompense it. The benefit which Christianity bestows on the State is a free gift, which cannot be repaid. The moment the State attempts to do this, either by patronage or by any kind of sanction or aid, it hinders and obstructs the proper work of Christianity. For Christianity deals with man as a free personality. As the grace which it announces and conveys is a free gift, so it must be freely apprehended and freely received by the soul to whom its overtures are addressed. External force can accomplish nothing. It was deliberately renounced and rejected by Christ as of no value in the kingdom of souls. The benefits of religion cannot be imposed by human enactment. Divine grace cannot be administered by human law. The might of embattled legions, the retinues of princes, the pageantry of courts, are worse than powerless to help forward the work of Christ; and all that States can do is equally useless for the same reason. For, the moment the State undertakes to deal with religious interests, it passes out of its proper sphere, and becomes a tyranny or an impertinence. Being merely a human instrumentality, organized and maintained to serve temporal and secular ends; confessedly unable to control any thing more than external conduct, — the only influence it can exert on conscience is either to oppress or debauch it. Nor is this all. Just as works cannot produce faith, but faith must produce acceptable works; so all attempts on the part of the State to assist Christianity by any methods which it can employ begin at the wrong end, so to speak, and work in the wrong direction, not with the course of grace, but against it. It is not too much to say, that the State cannot help Christianity. Whenever it has attempted so to do, it has inflicted an injury. It was not for nothing that Christ refused to even seem in any degree to solicit the favor or accept the patronage of the Roman civil power. Though in no sense antagonized to the Cæsar, yet he well knew that the Cæsar could send no legions to help him in the battle that lay before him. The kingdoms of this world cannot lend their powers to aid the unseen forces which exploit in the kingdom of God.

The most that the State can do to assist Christianity is, to refrain from interfering with it, and to protect it from all similar interference. The duty of protection may be "put on the same ground on which the prevention of disturbance is put in any other case where men are gathered in lawful assemblies." "The disturbance may proceed from enemies without, or ill-disposed persons within, the assembly. In either case it may be reformed by ordinary police regulations."[1] Manifestly, the extension of such protection is merely a civic duty, and does not in any way exceed the State's proper function, or constitute an intrusion into the proper domain of religion. The same may be said of all enactments which are intended to suppress or prevent crimes against religion, such as laws against sacrilege and blasphemy, and for the quiet observance of the Lord's Day. So far as these have a bearing on civil and social order, they are the legitimate subjects of civic enactment; but, so far as they relate to religion, the function of the State is strictly limited to the duty of protecting religion from such interference as would hinder or obstruct the free and proper exercise of it. The right of the State to

---

[1] Woolsey's Political Science, ii. 505.

deal with the property interests of religious corporations rests on the same grounds. Just in so far as the Christian Church deals with and employs the things over which the State has jurisdiction, it is entitled to ask of the State the protection of those things, and must submit them to the necessary and legitimate control of the State.[1]

The principles hitherto laid down enable us to determine by what method all conflicts between Church and State ought to be adjusted. We have seen that the two cannot rightly come in conflict. The one is a theocracy, under the rule of its divine Founder and living Governor. The other is a democracy, responsible to the people. The proper domain of each is wholly distinct from the other; there being but one term of relation, and but one point of contact; and that is, the individual soul. If, however, through mistaken or evil intent, the one be thrust into the domain of the other, the invaded interest is entitled to resist, and to rectify the frontier so to speak. Howbeit, each must resist with means and agencies appropriate to itself. The Church is not entitled to use force or to appeal to force. The Founder of Chris-

[1] Compare Woolsey's Political Science, vol. ii, pp. 506–508.

tianity himself determined this question in Pilate's judgment-hall, when he said, "My kingdom is not of this world: if my kingdom were of this world, then would my servants fight, that I should not be delivered to the Jews: but now is my kingdom not from hence;" and again when he said, "Put up again thy sword into his place: for all they that take the sword shall perish with the sword." Nor, on the other hand, is the State competent to wield spiritual weapons. Nevertheless, from the nature and necessity of the case, the State must be sovereign in its own sphere; and, therefore, from its decisions in regard to the bounds and limitations of its jurisdiction, there can be no appeal to any higher earthly kingdom or authority, since there is no higher. The Church is not a kingdom of this world, and has no jurisdiction in earthly matters. If, therefore, it ever should come to pass, as it often has in by-gone times, and as it notably did at the bar of Pontius Pilate, that the civil power should undertake to oppress or to smite the Church of God, the illustrious example of sacrifice is set for the Church to follow. The divine method of resisting encroachment and wrong, and of overcoming it, which Christ has commended for his Church to follow, is, not to appeal to force, nor to temporize and make terms with power, but is patiently to do the things which God commands, and, if need be, to die.

That there have been such conflicts in the past does not need to be stated. That such are even now impending has been pointed out. Though the evil of these, as we believe, may be largely neutralized; yet we dare not hope that we shall altogether escape, either the conflict or the evil. Much will depend upon the diffusion and acceptance of true views of the essential relation between Christianity and civil society. Much will depend, we venture to think, upon the influence which this Church shall exert as the historic and ethnic Church of this people, and as the single consistent upholder of the true authority of both Church and State; as the one teacher of the essential difference which divides them, and of the one relation which they sustain to each other. Should such ideas as this Church consistently and appropriately holds prevail, then we believe that a noble career in the domain, both of civil and religious liberty, lies before the people of this land. We believe, that while the distinction between Church and State would not be obliterated, but would, on the contrary, be more exactly defined, the apparent antagonisms, the actual contradictions, the possible conflicts, between them would become more and more rare, until they would cease altogether. We believe that each, acting freely in its own sphere, would support the other; religion strengthening the State by re-enforcing and dignifying the bonds which hold society together, and society cherishing religion as the great conservator of public peace and social order. Nevertheless, the condition is, that both must be permitted to act freely, each in its own sphere; the one being a kingdom of this world, the other a kingdom not of this world. The distinction between them lies in the nature of things, and shall not be abrogated till the new heavens and the new earth shall appear, wherein dwelleth righteousness.

It would be easy, perhaps, to indulge in optimistic anticipations, to prognosticate the growing harmonies, which, under the influence of the principles here laid down, shall charm away disorder in the world's fair future. But the thought which fills my own mind and heart, as I bring these lectures to a close, is, not of the Church's triumph, but of the Church's responsibility. If, indeed, the conclusions which we have reached are right, then the Church must do her work in the old way: there is no better. She must jealously guard against all worldly ambition. Her clergy must depend, not on their rank, or their state, or their prerogative; not on the positions of worldly influence, which are more and more temptingly held out to them, — but on the humility, the fidelity, the single-heartedness, with which they minister to the souls of men the things which belong to their peace. They must be content to be less and less men of the world, and more and more men of God. Moreover, the short and easy methods of official control, and of all kinds of mere institutionalism in education and charity, must be renounced; and a return must be had to the quiet, unobtrusive, patient methods of Christian nurture, domestic religion, and pastoral work in the homes and at the firesides of the people. Let us not deceive ourselves. The path of duty here indicated is arduous and unwelcome to the natural man. There are manifold temptations of ease, of pride, of sloth, to beguile us from it. The hearty acceptance of it would dismiss the Church for a time from that observation of men which, I fear, we are learning greatly to love: even as, in time of war, the promulgation of marching-orders breaks up dress-parades, and lays pomp and circumstance aside; while the battalions march in silence to the front to engage the enemy. To the more heroic but more obscure, to the more effective but less ostentatious, work and warfare of encountering evil in the human heart, of meeting it with spiritual weapons on the battle-field of the soul, of ministering to human needs and human helplessness, not merely in the temples of religion, but in the sanctuary of the home, the Church is now called by the obvious needs of the day and time; by the golden opportunities of the hour; by the richer promise of the future; by the secret motions of the Spirit; by the trumpet-call of our Leader and King, who, as he moves in the van of human progress, summons his Church away from the strifes and contentions of this world's kingdoms to a nobler contest and a diviner service in the cause of truth and for the kingdom of truth, the establishment of which alone works true and lasting good to man, — a good so true and so lasting, that it shall endure long after this world with all its kingdoms shall have passed away.

www.ingramcontent.com/pod-product-compliance
Lightning Source LLC
Chambersburg PA
CBHW031819230426
43669CB00009B/1192